# HOW TO WRITE THE MOST IMPORTANT LETTERS OF YOUR LIFE

## About the Author

In 1973, Meg Whitcomb originated the "Dear Meg" column, which established her as one of the country's most unique and inspirational advice authorities. Today she remains an important confidante to the 15 million people who read her column each week. Before becoming a household name, she covered international affairs at the UN and worked at *Life* magazine during its peak years in the fifties. Ms. Whitcomb lives with her husband and children in Bronxville, New York.

# "Dear Meg" tells you...

## HOW TO WRITE THE MOST IMPORTANT LETTERS OF YOUR LIFE

## MEG WHITCOMB

**WARNER BOOKS**

A Warner Communications Company

Names, people, places, incidents, and letters that appear in this book are either the product of the author's imagination or are used fictitiously. Any resemblance to actual events, locations, letters, or people, living or dead, is purely coincidental.

Copyright © 1986 by Meg Whitcomb
All rights reserved.
Warner Books, Inc., 666 Fifth Avenue, New York, NY 10103

W A Warner Communications Company

Printed in the United States of America
First Printing: May 1986
10 9 8 7 6 5 4 3 2 1

**Library of Congress Cataloging-in-Publication Data**
Whitcomb, Meg.      How to write the most important letters of your life.
    1. Letter-writing.  I. Title.
PE1483.W45 1986                    395'.4              85-29586
    ISBN  0-446-38210-8 (U.S.A.)(pbk.)
        0-446-38211-6 (Canada)(pbk.)

Cover Design by Don Puckey

To Arthur, who writes me the most important
letters of my life, with love.

# ACKNOWLEDGMENTS

A special note to Peggy Boomer and Dewey Yeager, who helped so much in writing this book.

# CONTENTS

# "Dear Meg" tells you...

# HOW TO WRITE THE MOST IMPORTANT LETTERS OF YOUR LIFE

# INTRODUCTION

Were you gazing out the window when your English teacher spent all of ten minutes explaining how to write a good letter? When your mother insisted that you write a thank-you to Aunt Maude for the wedding present, did it suddenly occur to you that you didn't know how? What about that letter you struggled over when you sent in your resume for the number one job on your list? Did you get it right?

We ask for many important things in our lives with letters—love, money, jobs, approval—and because a letter must say exactly the right thing, it must be handcrafted meticulously, like a finely tuned instrument. Today we often rely on word processors, computers, and other state-of-the-art machines that send messages whirring across the world in microseconds, but they don't take the place of the personal letter. *How to Write the Most Important Letters of Your Life* will teach you what your English class (or mother) didn't. It tells you what to say and, just as important, what not to say in a letter. It is not only a guide, but a permanent reference book you can pick up and refer to for just about any type of letter you want to write.

For you, the writer, a letter remains the one form of communication in which you are in complete control of your thoughts and feelings. A letter has power that machines do not. What kind of power? The power of persuasion and the power of permanence. For example:

—After a dozen phone calls, the acquaintance you loaned money to still hasn't paid it back. A letter explaining the courses of action open to you gives you leverage that a telephone conversation does not.

—Your old college roommate's father died and you don't know what to say. You haven't spoken for years and don't feel you can call. But a letter can express your feelings sincerely and gracefully.

—The love affair of the century is on the rocks and you're sorry. How many hours have you already spent hashing out hurts on the telephone? When one has to grapple with difficult feelings, often more can be said in two well-thought-out sentences than in hours of talking.

Letter writing is thought-provoking for the reader and gives the writer time to think things out carefully and thoroughly. It gives both parties a permanent record that can be emotionally savored or legally supportive for years to come.

Beyond the power and permanence of letters, there is the question of etiquette. Not so long ago the term *etiquette* was a bad word. In the counterculture years of the sixties and early seventies, "doing the right thing" was replaced with "doing your own thing," and at times it seemed that politeness had gone out the window along with neckties and sweater sets. Forgotten was the thank-you note, the letter of condolence, and other formal social communications. But the pendulum has swung and times have changed. The Conscientious Etiquette Objectors are sporting suits and ties, Social Graces are back in a big way, and Judith Martin's "Miss Manners" column is wildly popular across the country. There's no question that young people today want to know the niceties of social interaction.

Nowhere, perhaps, is the right thing more important than in the world of business. Architect Wilson Mizner used to say in his speeches, "Be nice to people on the way up because you'll meet them on the way down," advice that applies to every neophyte starting out in the business world. Good manners are good business, and a good letter can open doors (or shut them) in an acceptable way that the instant phone call or telegram cannot. Nobody can get a job without sending a concise personal letter—however brief—along with a resume. Nobody can get a line of credit without writing a letter requesting it. Nor can you enter into *any* business negotiation without putting your wishes in writing.

The written word oils the wheels of communication and enables us to deal with almost all of life's situations. The well-thought-out letter can solve problems, assuage guilt, declare love, ask permission, sell a product (or yourself), demand action, threaten, persuade, or cajole in a manner acceptable to everyone.

This book tells you how to write what could be the most important letters of your life. Communication is the way relationships are created, maintained, and ended. The ability to send clearly written messages, to be heard and understood, is central to any relationship—husband and wife, employer and employee, back-fence neighbors, business colleagues, parent and child, you name it. I hope this book will help you express your feelings on paper better than you ever have before.

# CHAPTER ONE

# THE RECONCILIATION LETTER
## HOW TO SAY YOU'RE SORRY

Good friends are hard to come by. It's been said that over a lifetime the average person acquires no more than half a dozen of the special kind of friend Cicero called "a second self." These are the people who don't have to be asked for help when times are tough. They sense your need and are there with everything they can offer. As columnist Walter Winchell put it, "A real friend is one who walks in when the rest of the world walks out."

Such close personal connections are few and far between, invaluable, and not easily replaced. When differences occur between friends, as they're bound to at one time or another, the very survival of the relationship can depend on finding a quick resolution. But sometimes that's not so easy and you have no idea what to say or even how to begin. What do you do? Write a letter.

When there's been an argument or any kind of falling-out, negotiation is needed to heal the rift. In some cases there's more than just an apology involved. Maybe, if only out of pride, you want to restate your position. Perhaps a compromise can be worked out. But your ultimate goal is to save the friendship, get it back on track.

There are many reasons why making up is best done by letter rather than in person or on the phone. Emotions can be too keyed up to allow for clear communication verbally. If you feel you can't think straight or get the words out right face-to-face, then sit down and write a letter.

When a friendship is in trouble, a letter enables you to be the first one to reach out with a conciliatory gesture while allowing you to maintain distance, or save face. You are making the initial effort, but with some reservation. You are testing the water, so to speak.

A letter lets you reveal yourself in a way that might not be possible in a verbal conversation. Some of the sentiments might be too delicate or sensitive. A thoughtful letter makes it easier. Plus, by writing a letter you are putting the ball in the recipient's court, and he or she is forced to think before answering. This gives your argument—or your apology—time to sink in. And you'll have a tangible record that can't be altered, as it could be in a face-to-face confrontation.

The fact that you took the time to write a letter is flattering. It's a deliberate act—not done in haste as with a phone call. A letter requires preparation and thought and represents a commitment that shouldn't be taken lightly. With lovers, the makeup letter may well end up with other treasured notes, bound by that special blue ribbon.

## Rules of the Game

1. *Plan ahead.* In preparing your letter, planning is essential. Start by lining up the points you want to cover. If the problem is a factual misunderstanding, some research may be needed to support your point of view. But don't overorganize and don't agonize over every word. That could stifle the spontaneity that is always helpful in expressing your sincerity. After all, it's not an essay for school or work, so better to let it flow naturally.

2. *Set the tone.* There should be a balance between firmness and gentleness. In dealing with a loved one, be tender. Be careful not to say anything that puts the recipient on the defensive, because then they'll be closed to your gesture of reconciliation. If there's any question about your letter being too strong, read it aloud. Or, if it's not too private, try it out on someone else.

3. *Tell the truth.* Honesty is the best policy, but telling the truth doesn't mean you have to tell *everything*. Accepting some blame or responsibility for the problem adds credibility. If an apology is in order, bite the bullet. Sometimes, too, you may want to couch the wording carefully out of consideration for the other's feelings.

4. *Write the letter promptly.* Don't let the problem smolder. Tackle it *fast*, no matter how difficult. You'll only feel guilty if you put it off, *plus* the letter will be harder to write. If you're responding to a reconciliation letter, delay in getting off your letter could diminish its relevance.

7

5. ***Don't ramble.*** Get to the point. Although brevity is stressed in almost every other chapter of this book, this is an exception. The length of your letter should depend on the situation, and you shouldn't feel any constraint in writing it. But it is important to stick to the point you want to make rather than straying off, which is easy to do when dealing with emotions. Rest assured your letter will be read carefully and thoroughly! As the college professor said about writing a paper, "Like a woman's skirt, it should be short enough to be interesting, but long enough to cover the subject."

6. ***Write it by hand.*** A handwritten letter is usually preferable, *providing your writing is readable*. An illegible scrawl won't advance the cause of forgive and forget one bit.

SOME EXAMPLES

The different kinds of makeup letters are as varied as the issues that cause them. Sometimes the most simple and trivial of misunderstandings leads to a breach in old friendships, which is what happened at the Sleekwood Country Club dinner dance one July evening.

The conversation at one table had turned to the Wimbledon tennis women's quarterfinals, which had been telecast that day. George Bright was one of the club's better tennis players and prided himself on being the authority on the spot. At one point he commented that it was a shame the play couldn't have been carried live, as was always the case with the men's finals. Mary Detail said she thought the telecast, or some part of it, had been live. George insisted that all of it had been taped. The fact that George had thoroughly enjoyed the cocktail hour contributed to the intensity of the argument.

Others added their opinions, but the focus was on George and Mary, neither of whom backed off. Then it happened. George, emphasizing his point with a sweeping gesture, knocked over a bottle of wine that spilled all over Mary's white dress. She hurriedly left the table, and the party. George's murmured apology was lost in the uproar that had followed. The next day, to top it off, George found out that he had been wrong about the quarterfinals. He wanted to call Mary to apologize but was frankly too embarrassed. His wife convinced him that a written apology was in order. Here is the letter that was enclosed with flowers and sent to Mary Detail the next day:

*Dear Mary:*

*This should have been a very simple apology, acknowledging that I was wrong about the quarterfinals. Of course you were right; the telecast was live.*

*But far more inexcusable was my ruining your evening and, perhaps, that beautiful dress. I have to confess I may have overindulged in the cocktail hour, but that doesn't excuse my behavior.*

*Arrangements have been made with the Sleekwood Cleaners to attempt to restore your dress. If that doesn't work—and they will advise me of the results—I insist upon replacing it.*

9

*Please forgive me, Mary. You have been responsible for teaching me several lessons that I won't forget.*

> *Your friend (I hope),*
> *George*

The letter, while brief, covered the important points—George reviewed the facts of the situation, admitted he was wrong, and apologized. Mary was touched by a humble side of George that she hadn't seen before.

Less easy to mend was the rupture between a pair of heretofore friendly neighbors. When Tom and Deidre Doting moved next door to Carl and Linda Laydbak, the couples took an instant liking to one another. Doubtless it was a case of opposites attract; the two families were as different as chalk and cheese. The Dotings' lifestyle was as programmed and perfectionistic as the Laydbaks' was casual, even chaotic.

The neighbors were further linked by the fact that four-year-old Angel, adored child of the Dotings', had a crush on six-year-old Lance, eldest of the Laydbaks' three rowdy boys. She could be seen all day long tagging along behind him, her blond braids bobbing over her starched pinafore.

One hot summer day Lance appeared at the Doting door to ask if Angel could come over and play in their backyard pool under the supervision of the Laydbaks' teenage babysitter. Mrs. Doting dressed her daughter in her bathing suit and sent her off with Lance.

You can imagine her state of shock when, an hour later, she came for Angel only to find the pool empty and the babysitter sprawled in front of the TV set with the two younger boys. Lance and Angel were nowhere to be seen. As the babysitter popped her bubble gum, she explained that Lance was confined to his room with ringworm, but that Angel couldn't be there because he wasn't allowed visitors.

The fact that the two youngsters were found playing happily in Lance's room only added fuel to Mrs. Doting's fury. In a curt telephone conversation that evening, she let Mrs. Laydbak have it in no uncertain terms, using words like "absentee mother," "criminal irresponsibility," and "neighborhood quarantine." The big chill became positively polar when Angel came down with a nasty case of ringworm herself.

The Laydbaks, recognizing that their unbuttoned ways had gotten them into a serious situation and could have even graver consequences, took steps to run a tighter ship. These included the prompt dismissal of the errant babysitter. Aware that, in terms of making up with the Dotings, the ball was definitely in their court, they decided to go for broke and try to heal the breach with a letter of abject apology. Here it is:

*Dear Tom and Deidre:*

*There's an old Irish saying, "You can live without your friends, but not without your neighbors." We are writing this in the hopes that we won't be in the unhappy position of having to do both, as far as you two are concerned.*

*First off, we regret from the bottom of our*

hearts the various screw-ups that resulted in our present unhappy situation.

How can we tell you how sorry we are that our sloppiness resulted in such a miserable experience for you two and Angel? We accept full responsibility and would give anything to undo the damage.

We've both been doing some heavy-duty thinking as to how it came about and have taken a number of steps to prevent any future problem. These include the firing of our so-called mother's helper and the imposition of stricter discipline all round. It was inexcusable that we didn't let you know about Lance's ringworm. We both thought the other had told you. That won't happen again.

You may well say that we're locking the barn door post-horse. But we want you to know how seriously we regard our commitment to more hands-on parenting. This incident may have changed our lives.

So we do hope you'll find it in your hearts to forgive us. Life on Latches Lane will be empty indeed without you all as friendly neighbors and neighborly friends. A thoroughly chastened Lance has written his own apology, enclosed for Angel.

Please think it over. If the answer is yes, won't you join us for a family barbecue next Saturday? If the answer is no, we'll understand.

Sincerely,
Carl and Linda

The letter worked. Why? Because it contained all the necessary factors that go into a sincere apology: honesty, good preparation (they apologized for everything that happened), and an unmistakable tone of sincerity. Finally, their invitation for Saturday gave the Dotings a fast and easy way to respond.

Probably the most delicate kind of apology is the one involving a love relationship. When a *faux pas* comes across as an insult to one or the other party, or, worse, if a third party poses a threat—real or imagined—a friendship can turn brown in a heckuva hurry. If, on the other hand, it is handled properly, it can survive.

Tina and Tom Tryout had been living together for five months when Tina's best friend, Sarah, asked if she could stay with them until she found a job and a place of her own. The answer was yes; Sarah moved into the guest room and proved the ideal houseguest. Until the day Tom lost his job and came home bombed. Sarah's was the only shoulder to cry on, so that's exactly what he did. But when Tina walked in she didn't see it that way. In less than an hour, despite Tom's protest and hasty explanations, Sarah was packed off. Two days later Tina found the following letter under her door:

*Dearest Tina,*

*I simply cannot let our friendship end over a foolish mistake. Although there's no way I would ever dream of disrupting your relationship with Tom, I have to admit that, had it*

*been me who walked in the door, I probably
would have reacted the same way you did.*

*Having lost a job myself just a few
months ago, I couldn't help but sympathize
with Tom. But letting him fall asleep with his
head in my lap was a dumb and unthinking
thing to do. I beg you to believe me when I tell
you that's all that happened. I hope you know
in your heart I would never do anything to
hurt you, dear friend.*

*Next to my family, your friendship is the
dearest thing in the world to me. I couldn't
bear it if you chose to end it because of my
foolish mistake. Please forgive me, Tina. I
want to make things right between us. Can we
talk?*

*With love,*
*Sarah*

Sarah laid it all out. She didn't mince words and
described feelings she couldn't possibly have expressed
face-to-face or by phone without breaking into tears. Her
sincerity, along with an honest plea for forgiveness, was
accepted by Tina as genuine because it was. The next day
their friendship was back on track.

## Putting It All Together

Making up can be a very rewarding experience, and
it isn't all that difficult. Just plan the points you want to

cover and let the writing flow naturally. Your tone should be sincere, your feelings honestly expressed, and your apology from the heart. Be truthful, even if it hurts. There's no ground rule for length; it depends on the situation. A handwritten letter is preferable, but that's not hard and fast. Most important, the quicker you get your letter out, the better you'll feel.

P.S. If you happen to be on the receiving end of a letter of apology, the kind thing to do is write a brief reply. Just enough to let the writer know all is forgiven and that the friendship is hereby back to normal. For example:

*Dear Doug:*

> *Your letter received, read and appreciated. Now let's get back to those skis we were going to buy together. I'll call you Saturday.*

> > *Dan*

Remember:
---

—*Plan* exactly what you're going to say and line up the points you want to make.

—Decide on the right *tone* for your letter.

—*Be honest.* (But that doesn't mean you have to tell the whole truth.)

—*Be prompt.* A late apology diminishes the impact of your letter.

—Write your letter *by hand* (unless your penmanship looks like chicken tracks).

# CHAPTER TWO

# THE COVER LETTER
## HOW TO APPLY FOR A JOB

The resume is typed and ready to go. Now all you need is a snappy cover letter that will convince your potential employer that you, and only you, are the person for the job. The cover letter is your first chance to sell yourself. For that's what job hunting is all about—a *selling* process with the cover letter helping to get the salesman's foot in the door and the resume providing the information for the sales pitch you're going to deliver in the interview.

The average person changes jobs five times in thirty years. One study puts the average number of Americans engaged in some type of job hunt or career switch at any given time at forty million. That's an awful lot of people wooing, winning, and (yes, sometimes) washing out in the great U.S. job follies.

In all fields it is essential for job applicants to present themselves in the best possible light. The final stage of the hiring process is generally a series of interviews, often starting with a minor personnel person and ending with a top executive. So "getting there"—to the personal interview with the right person at the right level in the right company—is the challenge.

This is where the cover letter is so important. It must attract attention and show the applicant as unique and desirable. Its job is to:

—close the gap between the abilities and experience of the applicant and the requirements for the job;

—introduce your resume in a way that relates it as closely as possible to the actual job specifications.

## Rules of the Game

1. *Brevity is key to the successful cover letter.* Think for a moment of the executive receiving it. Time is what he gives his company. Time is valuable to his employers and, of course, to him. The *brief* cover letter also demonstrates a skill that is valuable in any business. There's a saying that anyone can write a long document, but it takes talent to cover the same subject in a short one. So the brevity of the cover letter in itself is part of its selling power. Keep your letter to one page if you can.

   It is a good idea to leave certain information *out* of the cover letter, because it may limit your potential for the job. You should not necessarily include your age and a rundown of your experience. You may not exactly fit what the employer has in mind, so if these factors are brought out up front, they may work against you.

   Nor is it always necessary to explain *why* you want to change jobs. It is natural for an ambitious person to do so. An employer is more concerned with finding the right person than his reasons for wanting to change jobs.

2. ***The tone is all-important.*** As your employer's first impression of you, it characterizes you as an individual. The aim is to portray a dynamic, vigorous person, and that's *you.*

3. ***Have a clear idea of what you want to accomplish.*** Plan! Have a detailed picture of the person you're addressing. Develop a good mental image of how you can best fit the job description.

## Organizing Your Cover Letter

### Opening Paragraph

The opening paragraph accomplishes two things. First, it establishes the purpose of your letter—that you're interested in a specific job. Always mention how you learned about the job opening. Was it through an ad? A friend? The grapevine? Or maybe you read that something unusual was happening to the company—a reorganization, acquisition, personnel change, etc.

The opening paragraph also expresses a positive and (if possible) personal observation about the company or the individual you're addressing. These are turn-ons that immediately say yours isn't a form letter. Doing this may require a little homework, but it's worth it. Sources are available at your library. People close to the individual or company can also be helpful.

Here are three samples of good opening paragraphs:

*Mr. Geoffrey B. Parker, V.P. Marketing*
*Fabulous Foods*
*137 Fifth Avenue*
*New York, N.Y.*
*Dear Mr. Parker:*

*Fabulous Foods' recent acquisition of Chow Kong Oriental Foods suggests that there could be an opening in your marketing department for someone with gourmet food experience. The combination of FF's track record of five successive years of growth and the rapidly increasing public interest in ethnic foods, properly positioned, seems like a natural!*

*Ms. Jane O'Connor, Fashion Editor*
*STYLE Magazine*
*111 Lexington Ave.*
*New York, N.Y. 10011*
*Dear Ms. O'Connor:*

*Nancy Lane at SAVVY magazine has told me you are looking for a reporter with experience in fashion writing. I think STYLE is the best magazine in the field, and I'd like to talk to you about the opening when you have a free moment.*

*Mr. Samuel Sleek, Executive Vice President*
*Sterling, Goring, Waring & Sleek*
*420 Madison Avenue*
*New York, N.Y.*
*Dear Mr. Sleek:*

*Congratulations on your new advertising assignment from Future Motor Company. Advertising Age's account of the presentation you made in gaining this business was most impressive. The idea of a recreational vehicle with six wheels should revolutionize the ski country transportation market. Both have whetted my interest, as an agency automotive account supervisor, in participating in such an innovative effort.*

### Middle Paragraph

The middle paragraph of your letter should provide the opportunity to talk about *you!* It is here that you can *refer* to particular experiences from your resume that show why you are best suited to the job. But remember, no details! In other words, tailor-make yourself for the opening.

To do this, imagine yourself in the employer's shoes. Ask yourself, Why should I hire this person? What can he do for me? Why is he different from the other applicants?

Too many cover letters dwell on what the applicant expects from the job, rather than vice versa. In selling yourself—and that's the name of the game—keep in mind John F. Kennedy's words: "Ask not what your country can do for you; ask what you can do for your country." Here, and throughout your letter, be sparing with the "I" and "me" and focus on the "you."

21

---

Here are two samples of good middle paragraphs:

*With the advent of airline deregulation you must surely be interested in expanding your routes. My broad experience in acquisitions, especially in the travel field, could be valuable. Most recently, my department coordinated the Triangle Air acquisition by Universal, a project that provided me with useful insights into new directions the industry is taking.*

*As a fashion trendsetter, you must be eager to tie into the new "Graffiti Look." It's a trend similar to what we went through with the "Art Nouveau Look" in the seventies. I was very much involved with that design transition as head designer for Laura Best. As you know, we made it in a big way.*

### Closing Paragraph

The closing paragraph should convey your interest in the job and the employer, adding that you would genuinely like to work with him or her. It should also set up the next step. Since you are seeking an interview, here is where you take the initiative and offer to call for an appointment. Spare your prospect the time and trouble of responding by letter.

Some examples of good last paragraphs:

*I feel sure my degree in veterinary medicine and my work in animal research qualify me to run your boarding operation. I'm also confident my feeling for animals and desire to work with them set me apart from other candidates for the job at Samaritan Small Animal Hospital. Furthermore, Dr. Goodheart, I believe we share the same philosophy about preventive medicine for pets, and I'm eager to put it into practice under your direction. I will call your office for an appointment.*

> *Sincerely,*
> *Karen Kindness*

*As you can see, my career focus has been on communications planning. I'm sure my experience would make me valuable to you as your futures planner when Diatonics enters this new market. The prospect of working with the man responsible for the concept of consumer satellite telephone transmission is especially exciting. I'll call next week to set up a meeting where we can discuss this further. I hope your secretary can find some time on your calendar.*

> *Very truly yours,*
> *John Ready*

In short, a good cover letter needs three concise, informative paragraphs that lay your cards on the boss's table and make him look at them. Your resume does the rest.

SOME EXAMPLES

Ed Eager, twenty-eight, has had varied experience in the advertising field. At Williams, he sold space in the college paper and yearbook, and he spent two summers as a gofer at a local radio station. Ed enjoyed communicating with people and was also a sports jock.

So it was a natural that after graduation, armed with a crackerjack resume and the following cover letter, Ed looked to ad agencies for his first job. Media department work was the entry level area he chose as the training ground for managerial work. Here is his letter:

*Mr. George Fitzgerald, Personnel Director*
*Lodge Advertising*
*263 Beacon Hill*
*Boston, Massachusetts*
*Dear Mr. Fitzgerald:*

*I would like to talk to you about the job as a media trainee I saw advertised in the Globe. My familiarity with media stems from my advertising experience while I was at Williams and during summers, as outlined in my resume.*

*My background includes both media and selling situations. Most people feel that a good media person should understand selling tech-*

*niques as well. Let's hope my sales skills could be helpful to Lodge while I'm learning the agency ropes.*

*Your recent article in Pigskin Parade, "How to Keep Super Bowl from Becoming Stupor Bowl," was terrific. As an avid sports fan, I've been exposed to the outstanding work you're doing in the broadcast medium for clients, such as New England Telephone, and would welcome a chance to contribute as a member of your media team. Those commercials in the Celtics play-off game were out of this world!*

*I will be in Boston the week of June 15. May I call your office for an appointment?*

*Yours sincerely,*
*Edward Eager*

Ed got the interview and the job. His letter was enthusiastic and informative, and sold the boss on seeing him. Note that he immediately identified the job and how he learned about it. The middle and last sections showed a special interest in the agency's work and explained what Ed could do for the *company*.

Two years ago, Vicky Vivacious was a thirty-five-year-old homemaker with ten-year-old twin sons, a no-fault divorce decree, and memories of a three-year stint as a deejay and talk-show hostess on WTLK in Pittsburgh before she became a mother.

Vicky's child support couldn't make ends meet, so her aim was to get a job paying enough to take care of herself and the kids. Relying on her past experience in radio, she put out the word to friends in the business and kept a clear eye on the trade papers. But her chance came from an unexpected source. Here's her letter, short and to the point:

> *Mr. Joseph S. Wideband, Executive Producer*
> *WXYZ Radio, Inc.*
> *222 East 55th Street*
> *New York, N.Y. 10021*
> *Dear Mr. Wideband:*
>
> *I read in Liz Smith's column that Molly Mayfield is leaving her job on* People Are Talking *to be a full-time mother. Her show is a favorite of mine because it's so much like the show I had on WTLK Pittsburgh from 1974 through 1976.*
>
> *Liz said you were looking for a voice with a "new personality." My show,* Tunes and Talk with Vicky, *was especially popular because I developed it from a straight deejay show into a music and personality program with guests from both the music and theater worlds. A sort of music gossip column on the air, so to speak.*
>
> *It could be mutually beneficial to talk if you'd be interested. I'll bring along my tapes. May I call next week?*
>
> *Sincerely*
> *Vicky Vivacious*

Vicky told the producer just enough about herself to make him want more. Her resume filled him in on the details, but rather than mail him the tapes, she made it conditional that *she* go with them! Jobs that rely on a person's personality make an interview mandatory. Joe Wideband wanted to see how Vicky presented herself in person. He liked what he saw, auditioned her on an out-of-town station, and the job was hers.

P.S. Closing questions like Vicky's "May I call next week?" are not real requests for a reply. They mean the writer is going to call anyhow.

At another end of the spectrum is the college graduate looking for an entry level job. In this case, an interview can provide useful background information helping the graduate to gain information on a given field and company. Most firms consider such interviews part of their public relations and recruitment effort and are willing to devote staff time to them even if there is no immediate job opening. Here's a letter for such a "fishing" expedition:

*Ms. Eleanor Whiting, Personnel Mgr.*
*Connecticut Life Insurance Company*
*New Haven, Connecticut*
*Dear Ms. Whiting:*

*As a June graduate from Fairfield University, I'd like to explore a business career with Connecticut Life. I was most impressed with the training program your recruitment team outlined here on campus at Careers Day. My own research shows that new forms of insurance in a changing climate for the industry will make family protection and individual retirement income assurance more, not less, popular in the future.*

*As you can see from my resume, I graduated with a business degree in the upper third of my class. Among my extracurricular activities was membership in the Fairfield Debating Club, where I was the only woman.*

*My basic strengths are my interest in people and ability to work within a large organization. Connecticut Life is particularly interesting because of your reputation for advancing women. I look forward to proving the wisdom of that philosophy.*

*I will call your office to see when an appointment can be arranged.*

> *Very truly yours,*
> *Vera Classic*

Vera's letter showed that she had done her homework about the company and forged a link between her success as a woman on campus and Connecticut's policies.

Finally, there's the person who has been fired and is job hunting from home. He must face up to this situation because it will show up in his resume. Or, if the job exploration proceeds, a reference check will unearth it. He must be honest, but he needs a convincing rationale to explain why he left.

Fortunately for our hero, Steve Software was in the dynamic, fast-moving computer business. He was an engineer in research and development (R & D) with a medium-sized company, Silicon Valley style. He could assume that any prospective employer would understand the wild and woolly battles taking place in the industry's chaotic environment, where two new companies spring up for each one that goes bankrupt.

This case also demonstrates that trade jargon can help in specialized fields, adding credibility. Here's the letter:

*Mr. J. W. Whizzer, President*
*Nuevo Computer Company*
*Palo Alto, California*
*Dear Mr. Whizzer:*

*Nuevo's reputation for leading the pack in marketing as well as R & D is its main attraction for an EDP professional like me. In particular, your establishing a hotline to provide guidance for your home-computer customers was a real stroke of genius and surely helped sales.*

*As you can see from my resume, my five years of experience shows that I also have been on the leading edge of innovative research and development.*

*Actually, my concepts caused the parting of ways with Hot Shot Computers, where I advocated holding off our TR-12 until we had enough of a memory feature. Time proved me right because the TR-12 is in big trouble. Meanwhile, the company's marketing myopia has left customers confused and angry.*

*From what I know about Nuevo, my hands-on style of planning and research could add a competitive advantage to your operation.*

*I will call your office on Monday to see when we can get together.*

> Yours truly,
> Stephen Software

Steve had followed the guidelines as closely as possible under the circumstances, since he wasn't aware of a specific opening. He also made pluses not only of his experience with Hot Shot, but also of his departure from the firm.

## The Follow-Up Letter

You've had the interview and—let's hope—it was a breeze, creating a warm feeling between you and your prospective boss. But even if it wasn't all that great, a thank-you letter is a must. Repeat, a *must*.

Why? For many reasons. The first is common courtesy. The thank-you letter expresses gratitude to the busy executive for the time he has taken. After all, you should have benefited from that meeting in some way. At the very least, you had a practice session in interviewing, in itself very valuable. Many experts say that job hunters should deliberately schedule a few long shots before they go after the number one interview.

A thank-you also demonstrates efficiency and the ability to follow through. To reinforce that impression, the letter should go out promptly, while the interview is still fresh in the mind of the prospect.

A follow-up letter can also take advantage of a number of built-in opportunities. For instance, it's another way for you to separate yourself from other applicants.

The letter should capitalize on what you learned from the interview. You can reiterate those of your attributes that seemed most attractive to your interviewer and reinforce how they would benefit the company.

The thank-you note can provide an opportunity to send one or more copies of your resume for distribution to others in the organization. Most prospective employers like to get input from their colleagues.

Finally, the follow-up letter also confirms what you understand the next step to be. Who is next in the process? When and where is the next interview? Who sets it up, the company or you? Or maybe no specific next move came out of the meeting. Then *you* can suggest what should happen next.

Even if the interview didn't go well, your letter can accomplish other goals. It's a chance to repair any misunderstandings. Maybe he or she didn't realize how much responsibility you have in your present job. Use your gut instincts! It's not too late.

Don't underestimate one other possibility. Maybe you weren't among the front-runners for the job. But, as often happens, first choices often bow out or stumble. Perhaps the job was sixth on their list. Your reminder can then make you Johnny-on-the-spot. Clearly, the follow-up/thank-you can serve you well.

## Rules of the Game

What is the anatomy of a follow-up letter? Experience shows that it follows many rules of the cover letter. Basically, it's in three parts.

1. The opening offers thanks for the interview.

2. The "sell" section recalls the key points you want to reinforce.

3. "Re-thank"—it never hurts—and outline next steps.

The thank-you should follow the general writing rules for the cover letter, including brevity.

SOME EXAMPLES

> *Mr. Hugh S. Miller, Vice President*
> *Mile High Insurance Agency*
> *2215 Grand Street*
> *Denver, Colorado*
> *Dear Mr. Miller:*
>
> *Thanks for taking time from your busy day to meet with me yesterday. I was very impressed with Mile High's growth in the past five years.*
>
> *I was most interested in your recent entry into Group Casualty because of my own experience with the Underwriting Planning Department of the home office of State General in Hartford. Those six years convinced me that group coverage is little understood by many companies but, once understood, is very salable. With my State General background,*

*I'm sure I could be very effective in Sales with Mile High.*

*Your secretary has made an appointment for me with Mr. Grant next Monday. Thank you for setting this up. Again, I enjoyed meeting you.*

*With best wishes,*
*Howard Hotshot*

*Mr. John D. Gooding, Partner*
*Wild, Chase & Gooding*
*12 Wall Street*
*New York, N.Y.*
*Dear Mr. Gooding:*

*Meeting you yesterday was very stimulating and I appreciated your seeing me after hours.*

*The opportunity in your management training program is extremely interesting. My experience with Town Bank would seem quite complementary to the opening, since research and organization of data play important roles in both jobs. As you pointed out, working with people is an essential element in bond investing, and I believe I have demonstrated my ability in that area.*

*At your suggestion, I contacted Mr. Chase's office and will meet with him next Tuesday. Thanks for everything.*

*Sincerely yours,*
*Frances Friendly*

Note that both letters reinforce qualities believed to be important to the jobs.

## Putting It All Together

The job cover letter defines you as unique and desirable. Key points:

1. Tailor yourself to the job.

2. Don't give away too much.

3. Keep it short.

The follow-up letter is just as important. Key points:

1. Say thank you.

2. Restate your case.

3. Correct any misunderstandings that may have occurred during the interview.

4. Confirm what happens next, if anything.

REMEMBER:
—The opening paragraph should establish the job you're after and comment favorably on the recipient or company.
—The middle section draws from your resume special features that best meet the job requirements, briefly defining the relevance of your experience.
—The closing paragraph says you want the job and sets up the next steps.
—The follow-up letter is a *must*. In addition to

expressing thanks, it's your only chance to restate your case and correct any problems. The letter can also be used to confirm or suggest what happens next.

# CHAPTER THREE

# THE DEAR JOHN LETTER
## HOW TO SAY GOODBYE

In your heart of hearts you know its over. Really over. You've been trying to pretend it isn't but the old spark hasn't magically reignited. You have to face it; the flame is out.

So here comes the hard part—telling that super person you've been dating, engaged to, going steady with, or living with that it's finis, for good. But you want to do it in the kindest, gentlest, most diplomatic way possible. If your love affair had even a touch of what Jean Anouilh calls "the pleasure of the heart," it deserves a decent burial. Slithering away like a snake in the grass tends to make you feel like one. A clean break mends faster than a messy one.

So you ask, How do I do it? What do I say? And how do I say it right? Don't do what Joan Collins did when she went abroad for a month while her fiancé, producer George Englund, was slaving away in Hollywood. Ten days into her holiday she shot off a cable that said, "CAN'T SEE YOU ANYMORE STOP IN LOVE WITH SOMEONE ELSE STOP

VERY SORRY STOP LOVE  JOAN." While the cable got the message across, George was devastated. (And if you're into the gossip columns, you know that lesser blows have brought on more than one heart attack—and the urge to reach for the nearest .22!)

Joan's cable was a cop-out. She should have taken the time to sit down and write a Dear John letter explaining what had happened, why her feelings had changed, and offering a sincere apology. Plus—and this is important—she should have offered a few ego-boosting words, something that in effect would say, "You're great. This is *my* fault, not yours."

You, too, deserve the freedom from a guilt trip that a graceful exit gives. True, most of us duck the prospect of a scene (or, worse, more than one). That's why the disappearing act is such a tempting way out. But while sneaking silently offstage may avoid a scene, it causes more problems than it solves.

For example, unless you can afford to vanish for two months in Tahiti, how long can your answering machine make you excuses? How long can you duck into the nearest doorway when you see friends on the street? Or avoid your old haunts?

And there's the ultimately unpleasant aftermath: Shabby behavior on your part could well make your ex-lover fighting mad. After all, as Dorothy Parker used to say, "Scratch a lover and find a foe."

When mercy killing is the only solution to a terminal relationship, a Dear John epistle is gentler than a face-to-face meeting or a phone confrontation. Euthanasia by letter allows the dispatcher to think things out and plan what to say, rather than having to respond on the spot to tears, shouting, or even body blows.

In some cases, of course, a Dear John letter (for the sake of convenience I'm using the term for both men and

women) is actually welcome. When both parties feel the
end is near, it can be a relief for the receiver that he (or
she) doesn't have to do the dirty work. In these fortunate
situations, a Dear John is often cherished and laid away to
be reread in later years. There are plenty of these fading
mementos neatly tied with satin ribbon in dusty attic
boxes.

## Rules of the Game

To make your letter a decent *and* sensitive one, there
are three rules to follow.

1. ***Be straightforward.*** Don't beat around the
   bush. No doubt should be left, no loopholes over-
   looked that could provide grist for argument or
   appeal. If possible, point out a negative factor in
   your relationship that is *neither* one's fault as a
   lead-in to the nitty-gritty of your letter. You live
   too far apart, problems with children, cultural or
   religious differences—these are typical factors in
   blameless rifts.

2. ***Spare the other person's feelings.*** The easiest
   way to do this is to put the blame on yourself and,
   of course, apologize. Then offer an honest explanation for the parting. But, as you've seen in the
   chapter on making up, telling the truth doesn't
   mean you have to tell everything. (You never
   could stand his/her mother? Don't say it.) And
   your wording must be very carefully couched to
   spare hurt feelings.

> **3. End on a positive note.** Praise, compliment the person. Do a little stroking.

SOME EXAMPLES

George wanted out of his six-month romance with Wanda. One of the problems was Wanda's dependence and hero worship of George because she was seventeen years younger. She idolized him as a man of the world, which was flattering at the early stage of the romance but cloying as things progressed and Wanda started talking wedding bands. George had no desire to continue the relationship and wanted to let Wanda down as gently as possible. What he *didn't* want to tell her was that he had discovered a soulmate in Susan, whom he had met at a business luncheon. Susan was a Brazilian beauty with a high-powered job, and at thirty, her biological clock was ticking overtime. So George had no time to lose. Here's his letter:

*Wanda Dearest:*

*If you only knew how many times I have started this letter, how many times I have pictured you reading it. This is not an easy letter to write because honesty can be painful. But I must be honest. The truth is that I have nothing more to offer our relationship. Although the difference in our ages is not important now, I feel there will come a time when it may jeopardize our happiness.*

*As you may have suspected for some time, Wanda, I am simply not able to commit myself* to you. How I wish it weren't true, but at this point in my life I'm not ready to commit myself to anybody. Maybe this is why I've remained a bachelor for forty years. Maybe I'm just not _meant_ to be married.

Our six months together have been the happiest time of my life. You are the dearest, loveliest, most considerate woman I have ever known. Know that you will always have a special place in my heart. The man you choose will be envied.

George

Note that George applied all three principles of the thoughtful Dear John letter: he led off with the age factor, (nobody's fault), he put the blame on himself, and then he stroked.

It is important not to overdo the velvet-glove treatment. Following is a letter that didn't work. Nice guy Nick and preppy Patty met when he was a senior and she a sophomore at Hiram Walker State. They were a hot item all through his senior year; then he returned to his hometown to job-hunt while Patty continued on at school. As time passed, Nick knew that Patty wasn't for him, but she was bombarding him with letters, phone calls, and invitations to football games.

Then Patty told him she had won a scholarship to study for a year in Italy, so he thought he'd found a painless way out. Wrong.

*Dear Patty,*

*This is a tough letter to write because it may upset you, and you know I never want to hurt you. But when you called Tuesday to express your doubts about going abroad, I was forced to do some heavy thinking. Especially because you sounded so hurt when I agreed that you should take advantage of such an important scholarship.*

*I realize it's not fair to either of us, but most of all to you, to let things drift the way they are. You may not realize it, Patty, because I've never been much good at confiding, but right now my life is really up in the air. A job is beginning to look like an impossible dream, I'm not sure where I'll end up settling down, and I'm even beginning to doubt if the computer business is right for me. To say that my life is in limbo right now would be the understatement of the year.*

*But the long and the short of it is that I'd feel very guilty if I tried to tie you down in any way. Your year abroad should be a no-strings deal. After all, you're going there to know the people—and you can't do that if you're always thinking about me. I'll always be grateful for the wonderful times we've shared, and I mean that from the heart, Patty. I'll always want to stay in touch. Please send me a postcard, and maybe when you get back we can get together for a drink or something.*

*As ever,*
*Nick*

Nick's letter was going great until the last paragraph. Send a postcard? Go out for a drink? No way. Nick committed the deadliest Dear John sin—he left the door open.

The response was swift and disheartening. Two fifty-dollar theater tickets and an invitation to Patty's birthday dinner arrived in the next mail. The message was: "I'll wait as long as it takes."

Janice, however, had more luck in ending her short-term fling. She's a junior executive at a business consulting firm in Boston. At twenty-nine, she's been married to Hal for three years, and someday they might have kids, if it doesn't get in the way of their lifestyle—weekend sailing or skiing.

Janice's boss is Ted, forty, a junior partner and happily married, with a wife and two kids. It's obvious that he has a bright future.

Janice travels a lot—occasionally with Ted—for major client meetings. The attraction they felt for each other soon got out of hand. Drinks together after a tough day in Minneapolis, or St. Louis, or Los Angeles soon grew into an affair that continued for three months.

Then, almost simultaneously, both realized that what initially might have seemed just an innocent adventure could eventually cause big personal and professional problems. While Janice wrote the Dear John letter, it might just as well have come from Ted:

*Dear Ted,*

*This hurts, but please hear me out. Recently it dawned on me, as it probably has on you, that what we felt was an innocent fling isn't right for either of us. I guess we were the victims of circumstance. You are not only a beautiful guy, but one whose professional talent I greatly admire. I'm sure it was my fault for starting things, and for that, I'm very sorry.*

*I know how much you love your wife and children and what a great life you have with them. Most people would sell their souls for your family and business success. You're one very lucky guy, and I'd never forgive myself if I were the one to make you press your luck too far.*

*I know you will understand, Ted, why I've asked for a transfer to John Jaffe's group. As you know, he's considered tops in his area and that will be a real challenge for me. Incidentally, I've also made an appointment with a marriage counselor to make sure that from now on I put my emotional energies where they belong—at home. You will always be special to me, Ted. Good luck and God bless.*

*Janice*

There was a lot in this short letter—flattery, admission of guilt, shouldering the blame, and, last but not least, Janice's sensitive but *final* way of ending their relationship.

Here's a case where romantic Rory, an idealistic young reporter who has scored several exclusive newsbeats uncovering local government corruption, is transferred to the city room of a large metropolitan daily. The appealing newcomer from Smalltown is immediately taken up by high-powered Helen, the paper's sleek, smashing Lifestyles editor. Helen introduces him to life in the fast lane—gallery openings, sneak previews, the best tables at the "in" restaurants, and dancing till dawn. Rory falls hard, pursues her with flowers, letters, and many offers to meet her family. But to no avail.

A year later, Helen still eludes him, refusing to give up the other men in her life while declaring eternal devotion to Rory. She's pettish when deadlines make him late for dates and begins deliberately taunting him with her attentions to another handsome newcomer.

Rory finds his work as well as his emotional health slumping, so he decides to take the end of the affair into his own hands. Here's Rory's letter:

*Dearest Helen,*

*You don't know how hard it is for me to write this. I hardly know where to start. Maybe I should just say that I feel our relationship, great as it's been, has turned into a dead-end street. And dead-end streets were never my thing.*

*As a newspaperman, I'm lousy at expressing myself in matters personal, so I'm going to resort to some back-home philosophy instead. Out there, when things get tough, we know how to cut our losses. So as much as I hate to lose you, I can't continue seeing you anymore. I can see your life is full right now, and I suspect you've been too kind to come right out and level with me about your true feelings.*

*I'll never forget our magical moments*

*together, but I'd rather have those golden memories than continue the way we are. As I get on with my life, I wish you only happiness in yours.*

*Rory*

Although Rory was brokenhearted, he didn't let it show. His letter showed kindness as well as objectivity. And he was honest. Though he didn't place the blame on Helen, she'd have to have rocks in her head not to get the message.

Everyone thought that Jerry and Pat were the ideal couple, well suited to each other, outgoing, and fun-loving. With his all-American football background, Jerry was a natural for his sales job in Chicago and all the wining and dining that went with it.

Pat continued her free-lance design business when they married, three years after they started living together. Her income helped to give them the affluent lifestyle they so enjoyed, and also got her out of the house.

But then she finally talked Jerry into their having a baby, someone he could play football with someday. She took that tack because Jerry was the type who had to be sold. But it didn't work out. Though he showed little interest in the baby and came home at all hours of the night after wild times in the Windy City, he insisted their marriage was good.

But Pat decided, after a futile counseling attempt, that it wasn't working and she wanted to start over while she was still young enough to pursue her design work and, with any sort of luck, find an attentive father for little Tony. Here is the letter she had delivered by messenger to

Jerry while she and Tony were out of town with her parents:

> *Dearest Jerry:*
>
> *I have to believe that this won't come as a terrible shock. While you claim to want a life together, we've drifted further and further apart. And the efforts to make a real home for Tony and me just haven't worked out.*
>
> *You're still the fun-loving Touchdown Kid that wowed them at U. of T., and I have great memories of those days. But no matter how hard you try, your best of times will always be with the boys and that sort of easy-come, easy-go life. Unfortunately, we both realize now, as we should have sooner, that there isn't room in that world for Tony or me full time.*
>
> *We can make our plans through Tom Delahanty, who will be handling the divorce for us. He understands that I want to make this as painless as possible. He will be in touch with you in a few days. You'll always be Tony's father, even if you and I aren't man and wife.*
>
> *Always,*
> *Pat*

The end-of-the-marriage Dear John letter cannot, of course, take the place of further meetings because divorce seldom works that way. But it *can* lay the foundation for a less painful break because it sets the stage for further talks in a less emotional way than would a face-to-face confrontation.

## Putting It All Together

Whatever your reason for ending a romance—from boredom to broken promises—a Dear John is the kindest way to take your leave. You'll achieve a parting that's permanent, yet as painless as possible.

### *Remember:*

When organizing your letter, don't forget the following rules:
- —Be up front and aboveboard. Try to find an objective reason for ending the affair that is beyond the control of either of you.
- —Lower the pain threshold by taking the blame for the breakup and apologizing for your failings.
- —Massage the bruised ego with a tender touch. Accentuate the positive in the other person and focus on a brighter future.
- —Don't lie. You want to be able to live with yourself.
- —Don't leave the door open—not even a tiny crack.

# CHAPTER FOUR

# THE DEAR JOHN BUSINESS LETTER
## HOW TO END A BUSINESS RELATIONSHIP

There are times when a business association turns sour and you know you have to do something about it. But what? Does the falling-out require that you fire a firm? Warn them? Or just use some friendly persuasion to try to get them back on the track? Whichever it is, when the phone calls and complaints have failed to get action, a Dear John letter is definitely in order.

Unlike the unpleasant task of dismissing an in-house employee—which is always done in person (or should be)—a letter is the best way to handle a faltering business situation. Why? Because in business there are tangible considerations such as contracts, renewal dates, amounts of money, instructions, and agreements involved that must be put to paper. You probably committed all the details of your relationship to writing at the start of the business deal, so spelling out the problems now will help reduce the possibility of misunderstanding.

An explanatory letter has other pluses, too. It lets the recipient read the entire presentation without being able to interrupt your train of thought. Similarly, it gives him or her plenty of time to check his facts against yours and present a coherent, documented reply. A letter also spares you his initial reaction, which could be anything from anger to indignation—or worse.

The three most common business situations where a Dear John letter is used are

—when you want to terminate a business deal. This is usually an impersonal letter explaining why you no longer want to continue using a firm's services;

—when you want your letter to act as a negotiating tool. You are disturbed about something the recipient of your letter is doing (or has done) and want to improve the situation;

—when you want the relationship to survive, but want to improve operating conditions.

## Rules of the Game

1. *Be persuasive.* Persuasiveness is a common requirement in all three situations. The recipient must understand and appreciate *why* a business relationship is in trouble. He may not agree with you, but at least he'll know your reasons. (This will also help your image if he complains to a higher power, or even to friends.)

2. *Your letter must be based on factual documentation.* The better the documentation, the easier

your job of persuading will be. And if you are willing to accept some of the responsibility for your part in creating the problem, it will add to your credibility.

3. *Anticipate the recipient's arguments.* If you have a pretty good idea of how the recipient of your letter is going to respond, if you feel you have a leg up on his reactions, you can deal with them in your letter.

4. *End on an upbeat note,* even when the relationship is truly over. Assure the person that his future looks bright, even if you don't mean it.

SOME EXAMPLES

There was no doubt in Fred Fussy's mind that his supplier, Acme Ingredients, had to be fired. As head of purchasing for Super Puddings, Inc., he knew that if he let Acme screw up one more time, it would be his neck as well as theirs.

Acme had sent two shipments of pudding mix made with cyclamates instead of saccharin, and had missed four delivery dates in less than eight months. Fred's complaints had gone unheeded, so it was time to act. Here is his letter:

*Mr. George Quota, V.P. Sales*
*Acme Ingredients, Inc.*
*24 Railroad Ave.*
*Albany, N.Y.*
*Dear George:*

*I'm sorry that it is necessary to write this*

*letter, but Acme's performance on Super Pud-dings' business leaves me no alternative. I doubt, George, that you'll be surprised by our decision to discontinue Acme as a supplier.*

*This was not a hasty decision. We have conducted an extensive review of Acme's past performance. This included the four late deliv-eries, which closed down our lines twice. Note the enclosed copies of correspondence dealing with that.*

*But even more serious are the two occa-sions (January 10 and April 15) when cycla-mate formulations were received. Fortunately, our Quality Control Unit caught both slipups. Otherwise, Super Pudding with cyclamates could have gotten on the market, risking a massive recall at a cost of millions of dollars to us. My letter to you of January 11 (copy attached) alerted you to the seriousness of this, and what a repeat performance would mean.*

*I have personally enjoyed working with you and recognize that you are in a tough spot. Let's hope that your people learn from this experience and adopt tighter processing controls.*

> *Very truly yours,*
> *Fred Fussy*

It was an open-and-shut case. Fred documented Acme's past mistakes in detail and explained the serious-ness of the errors, and he cited earlier warnings of the consequences should another error occur. Lastly, he closed with a practical point regarding Acme's performance.

The next case involves firing an employee. The actual act should be done face-to-face in a very personal, sympathetic way—cushioning the blow as much as possible. A letter should follow confirming specific arrangements—notice, termination date, benefits, etc. Also, legal implications must be considered. There have been many Equal Opportunity Employment Commission discrimination cases that could have been avoided had the conditions and reasons for termination been spelled out in writing.

In preparing for the dismissal meeting, you should spend as much time as you did in hiring the individual. Actually, there should have been plenty of warning to the employee that this was coming, assuming you held frequent, regular performance reviews and advised that the job could be at risk unless there were improvement. You might even have set an improvement deadline for which the clock has now run out.

Our letter deals with the real estate firm of Hunt & Search, headed by Michael Mortgage. Two years earlier he had hired Sally Grind. She was attractive, in her thirties, and spent a lot of time on the job. Hunt & Search's system of giving each person a fair share of prospects had given her many sales opportunities. Additionally, Michael went overboard in supporting the women on the staff, feeling that in many cases they could better sense home-buying needs than could the men.

But it wasn't working out. Sally just wasn't making it. At the first two six-month performance reviews, he had gone easy on her, figuring she needed more time to learn the ropes. At the last review he opened up and expressed his concern. He noted complaints from several prospects about her brusque approach. One claimed that Sally had said, "Take it or leave it."

That's a no-no in the real estate business, so Michael prepared himself thoroughly for the dismissal session, both out of fairness for Sally and because of his Equal Opportunity concerns about firing a woman. This letter, which he gave Sally at the end of their twenty-minute meeting, contains the main points he made:

> *Ms. Sally Grind*
> *247 Cactus Drive*
> *Palo Alto, CA*
> *Dear Sally:*
>
> *I'm taking this action as much out of concern for you as for Hunt & Search. With your sales performance on our commission system, the company isn't making enough money, but neither are you. I expressed this at our February review, at which time you agreed to work on your "people tactics." I believe you have tried to do that over the past six months, but unfortunately it hasn't changed things.*
>
> *As we discussed, there are "people" people and "numbers" people. I remember our first interview when you mentioned you sometimes had trouble dealing directly with customers, and I wish I had gone into this further with you. But your desk work and mathematical know-how have been excellent—better than anyone else's at your level in the office. I've noticed that many of our people come to you for advice on mortgage financing.*
>
> *The attached will provide you with the*

*details of the separation. Note that you will have salary support for the next month and that your medical and dental insurance is continued six months. There is also a letter of recommendation I have drafted that you may use according to your own discretion. My friend Bill Sawbucks at Home Finance has expressed considerable interest in you. He has been looking for someone with real field experience in mortgage planning.*

*I'll be following your career, and if there's anything further I can do to help, don't hesitate to call me.*

*All the best,*
*Michael*

Your business associate has made a major error that could lead to the dissolution of the relationship. You want to take advantage of the crisis to improve existing conditions. If the negotiation is successful, you've made a significant step forward. Otherwise, it's all over. Usually under these conditions, the party at fault has more to lose by the dissolution.

Such was the situation in the client–advertising agency relationship between Harry Square, V.P. of Advertising at Union Motors, and Tom Headline, who was the top man on the Union business at Rockum, Sockum & Ketchum (RSK). The association was twenty years old, and RSK had produced topflight ad campaigns for Union. Their creativity was known to be among the best in the business, and their introduction of the new Jay Bird model three years ago had been a smashing success.

While RSK was a great creative shop, their accounting was mediocre at best, and this was a continuing irritant to Harry and Union Motors. Every month there was some sort of a billing flap. Harry would call this to Tom's attention—almost always in writing—and eventually it would get straightened out. But Tom acted as if he were above the details of accounting, with his attention focused on the big picture of creating great advertising.

Such was the scenario when the scandal occurred. While it related to the mundane world of sales promotion, the fact that the auditors found that the mighty RSK had been double-billing Union off and on for three years made headlines in the advertising press. Against this background, Harry carefully planned this letter:

*Mr. Thomas Headline, Senior V.P.*
*Rockum, Sockum & Ketchum, Inc.*
*385 Michigan Ave.*
*Chicago, Illinois*
*Dear Tom:*

*While we have spent considerable time unraveling the sales promotion billing problems, no long-term solution has been offered by you or your people. And, of course, the problem is not a new one. (Note the attached summary of the thirty-two different misbillings over the past two years.) It's just that no one at RSK seems to be responsible for billing us, even though as a $60 million client, a lot of money is involved.*

*Now my management is very concerned. They've heard from many of our stockholders and are asking how responsible we are. There have been questions about Union's agency assignments and whether we should have an agency review. It's that serious, Tom.*

*All of us appreciate the fine job your people do in creating and placing advertising for us, and how personally involved you are in that. And I don't want to change that by diverting your attention from directing those efforts.*

*Clearly it would make sense to have someone assigned to our account who would have no other responsibility than billing. Ideally, it would be a senior person with a financial background who could review your procedures and devise means of streamlining them.*

*I'm looking forward to hearing from you.*

*Cordially,*
*Harry*

Harry's letter worked like a charm! The possibility of losing the blue-chip Union account registered in a big way. Especially since the billing problems and Union management's concern were amply documented. At the same time, Harry had done some stroking, complimenting Tom on the quality of RSK's advertising.

The result? The agency assigned a qualified financial person to the Union account at the V.P. level. Under his watchful eye, the accounting problems disappeared.

The relationship between High Spirits Distillery and its distributor, Blended Best, Inc., was even longer and closer than Union's with RSK. It went back to Prohibition when the heads of both companies worked together rum-running from Canada to the States. Those were rough-

and-tumble days, and the bonds of friendship between Abe Premium and Mike Best were the strongest. It was this relationship that was handed down to their sons, now running their respective companies.

Young Hal Premium was a marketing genius, and under his leadership High Spirits had dozens of successful new brand introductions, not easy in the liquor business because of tight government regulations. The one fly in the ointment for Hal was the lack of cooperation he was getting from one distributor, Blended Best. The company was headed by Max Best, who was apparently more interested in the horses than in doing a good job for High Spirits.

This made it awkward for Hal, not only because of the family legacy, but because state law dictated that liquor distributors could be fired only by successful legal action. Under these circumstances, here is the letter he wrote to Max:

*Mr. Max Best, President*
*Blended Best, Inc.*
*12 Crab Walk*
*Baltimore, Maryland*
*Dear Max:*

*This is a difficult letter to write because of the close ties you and I and our families have enjoyed over the years. I particularly enjoyed our business relationship when you were personally handling Blended's marketing—remember the 300-case floor display of Golden Club you put up at Discount Booze? People could barely get into the store, let alone miss that display!*

*But all that seems to have changed. The latest sales report for High Spirits' 103 distributors shows Blended Best dead last. Average bottle facings were two versus our national average of five. There were shelf talkers in only 12% of your stores against the national average of 67%. So it went for floor displays, promotional advertising, etc., as documented on the attached.*

*My Marketing V.P. and product managers are climbing the wall. They insist we need a stronger Maryland distributor—one who will really promote our brands. Of course, under Maryland law, we would have to take you to court and prove the lack of performance, which I would hate to do.*

*So Max, I'm asking you for old times' sake to step in and direct Best Blend's marketing the way you used to. I'll give you a call next Tuesday to get your response.*

> *As always,*
> *Hal*

Hal had done his homework, documenting Best Blend's poor performance. The not-too-veiled threat of taking Max to court to end the distributorship was all the persuasion needed. All of this was softened by praising Max's marketing ability. The negotiation put Hal in the position of being able to go either way—fire Max or get a commitment for improved performance.

It turned out to be the latter. Max personally took on the marketing leadership, and in less than two years, Blended Best was one of the top High Spirits' distributors.

Let's say you don't want to end a business relationship, but there's a specific problem that needs to be solved. Because of close personal ties involved, the issue is best dealt with in a letter to avoid embarrassment. Also, the letter indicates how serious the problem is. Here's an example:

Dick Invest and Jerry Hottip had been close friends since their school days, with each being the best man at the other's wedding. To top it off, their wives hit if off very well, which was fortunate because they were next-door neighbors in fashionable Larchmont, New York. Their relationship even extended to business, where Dick Invest, at Shapiro Brothers, was Jerry's best corporate bond customer. The amount of business conducted between them made Jerry one of the top brokers at High Level.

What could be a problem in this relationship? While on the surface it seemed minor, the fact was that Jerry had turned argumentative. He was showing signs of extreme fatigue and his performance was slowing down. He began getting bond quotations wrong as well as late, and Dick had covered for his mistakes more than once. In addition, Dick knew Jerry was borrowing money—he'd loaned him two thousand dollars himself, no questions asked—and that he was getting deeper in debt. He suspected a drug habit, and when he saw Jerry snorting a line of coke in an upstairs room at the country club dance, his suspicions were confirmed.

How to warn Jerry that not only his health but his business with Shapiro Brothers was in jeopardy? He thought about doing it over lunch, or even over the back fence. But that wouldn't convey the seriousness of the problem. So he put together the following letter:

Mr. Jerry Hottip
High Level, Inc.
120 White St.
New York, N.Y. 10017
Dear Jerry,

You're wondering why I'm writing a letter when almost all of our contact is face-to-face or by phone, right? Okay, here's why. I want to get this all out without any flak from you, dear friend.

The bond quotations you've been sending over have been erroneous over 30% of the time in the past two months. They have also been late. I've bailed you out most of the time, but I can't cover for you indefinitely. The company has lost out several times because of your mistakes, and I'm getting heat from the front office. I've tried many times to get the urgency of the problem across to you, but it hasn't registered. Now I know why.

Jerry, my heart went out to you when I discovered you were doing cocaine at the dance the other night. You know your secret is safe with me, but I cannot stand by and watch you go downhill without saying something. Your job, at least with us, to say nothing of your health, is at stake here. I beg you to get help and will be more than happy to give you a hand. Pardon the cliché, but I know whereof I speak.

Remember my little sister Sara who moved to California when she graduated? Smart little Sara who always got straight A's (as well as all the boys) and could do no wrong?

*Three years ago Sara lost her job at WXYZ-TV because of her coke habit, proving you don't have to be dumb to be a druggie. Sara got well at a wonderful rehab place in New Jersey and has been fine ever since. She has a new job and is active in her local Narcotics Anonymous group. So there is help out there, friend. All you have to do is ask for it.*

*I want the old Jerry back on the job before there's no more job to go back to. Let's talk soon.*

*Yours,*
*Dick*

Dick's letter was a highly personal appeal. The persuasion came through his close personal relationship with Jerry and wisely omitted any intimidation or reference to carrying the problem to a higher-up. Confidentiality in itself can be a positive factor in dealing with problematic business dealings. The guy on the spot appreciates it and is usually inspired to correct the problem.

## Putting It All Together

The Dear John business letter can be a very effective tool with the right amount of friendly persuasion.

*Remember:*

—Be persuasive.
—Document the problem as best you can.

—Anticipate the recipient's response and deal with it
in your letter.

—Accept *some* responsibility for the problem if you
can find a way to do so. It softens the blow.

# CHAPTER FIVE

# THE CREDIT LETTER
## HOW TO PLAY THE CREDIT GAME—AND WIN

"Don't borrow trouble; borrow money, and trouble will come of its own accord" has been the time-honored attitude toward getting into debt.

But times are changing. In today's consumer-driven society, credit is not simply a convenience. It's an essential tool for getting the necessities as well as the good things of life. It's one of the best ways of beating inflation, to boot. So whether you want to get a phone or electric power hooked up, rent a car or a hotel room, join a book or a record club, buy a couch or a car, finance a college education or a cottage with a picket fence—you're a potential borrower.

Forestalling trouble is the reason why *written* communication regarding credit is so important. I stress *written* because any dealings involving money *must* be put on paper, both to prevent misunderstanding at the time of the transaction and as a record for the future.

But, first off, some words about the safe and successful use of credit.

In making decisions about extending credit, most lenders look for what I call a "triple-A" rating in a borrower. They weigh three factors in evaluating you as a credit risk: *ability*, *assets*, and *attitude*.

*Ability* consists of your capacity to pay back your loan, the difference between your income and spending patterns, plus other liabilities.

*Assets* are those tangibles that represent your financial worth and could, in a pinch, be used as security against money advanced. They range from possessions, such as a house or car, to monetary nest eggs like life insurance and/or bank accounts.

*Attitude* is a state of mind, reflected in your record of repayment of debts. It can be the most important factor in deciding your triple-A rating. It requires that you have shown both consistency and responsibility in paying your financial obligations on time and in full. Evidence of a sound attitude can often tip the scales in your favor.

If you bear in mind the importance of being able to present yourself as a triple-A credit risk, all your written communications regarding credit will be easier and more effective.

## Rules of the Game

Here are four important rules that apply to all applications to lending institutions asking for credit.

1. *Be straightforward.* Provide the facts in a sincere, nondefensive manner. Don't gild the lily,

but do include all positive, relevant facts. Remember, bullying doesn't work. It puts the lender on the defense.

2. *Keep it brief.* Long, drawn-out letters generally find their way to the bottom of the analyst's pile.

3. *Show stability and consistency* to generate credibility. If there isn't room on the application, include the favorable facts in an attached memo.

4. *Direct the letter to the right person,* typically a credit manager or loan officer. Don't send it to the CEO. That will cost you time because he'll just send it on to the proper channel.

## Establishing Credit

Anyone trying to establish credit for the first time quickly discovers it's a catch-22 proposition. It's like the no-win quest for that first job where you're turned down because you lack experience. Yet the very experience you need can only be gained if you get that first job.

So it goes with creditworthiness. It presumes you already *have* a credit history. But how can you have a good credit report when you're just making the first move toward building one?

Paradoxically, your first step toward creating the triple-A credit rating is to apply for credit—a bank MasterCard, American Express, Visa, or other major credit card. To do that you'll need a steady job paying $10,000-plus, a checking account with no history of overdrafts, and a savings account to which you add regularly, totaling $3,000 or other assets, such as a C.D. (Certificate of

Deposit), stocks, or bonds in that amount. It's worth borrowing part of that initial capital from a family member or friend (see Chapter 6 on how to get such a personal loan) to start you on the road to creditworthiness.

Now let's look at the type of information you'll need to supply in applying for a credit card using a form supplied by the bank or charge card company.

First, provide the facts about yourself—your name, age, social security number. Your marital status is necessary only if you're applying for a joint credit card, or an account with your spouse.

Give your address and your employer's name and address. If you've been less than three years at your current residence and/or job, you'll need to supply information on previous ones.

Tell what your income is, breaking it down by job paycheck and other sources. Your bank accounts should be included.

List all your financial obligations, including your rent and/or mortgage payments, outstanding bills or debts, and your progress in paying them back. Other relevant information includes whether you are a guarantor on other debts (for example, if you have co-signed a loan for someone else). You must also list alimony or child support payments you're making.

Once you have received your charge card, begin to establish a credit history by using it regularly and paying the bills promptly. You can advance the cause by adding other credit cards for gasoline, phone service, and department stores. Be sure to maintain a perfect payment record and be careful that your installment debt outstanding never exceeds 15 percent of your gross income. This is regarded as prudent by most financial counselors.

You can then add an important string to your credit bow by taking out a savings passbook loan, which you can invest in a C.D. or other financial investment at a higher rate of interest. You'll pay it back on time, of course.

Now you have done everything you can to prepare yourself for the next step in most people's credit lives: the unsecured loan request.

SOME EXAMPLES

There are two basic types of loans made by banks and other lending institutions. The *secured loan* is backed by some form of collateral, such as a car, house, or furniture, and the interest rate is lower than on the unsecured loan.

The *unsecured loan* carries a higher interest rate because there is no security that can be repossessed if the loan isn't repaid.

There are many types of lending agencies, from prestigious banks to finance companies. All are regulated by laws that vary from state to state. Most require the borrower to pay for the credit application, which costs between ten and twenty-five dollars to process. Some, like those in New York, make the lender pay the cost of the credit examination. Most credit applications go through credit bureaus that check out your credit history.

Lenders actually are in business to lend money, despite their image of being supercautious. To make money, they have to put their money to work. Many, such as banks, have shareholders who want a return on their investment. So they have to be careful.

In addition to the information required in applying for a credit card, a letter or application requesting a loan will also include several other pertinent facts. These include the purpose of the loan, the name and address of your nearest relative, the year and make of your car (if you own one), and whether you have ever been subject to any financial judgments, garnishments, bankruptcy, or other legal proceedings.

Here is a typical letter applying for an unsecured bank loan:

*Mr. Elmer B. Eagle, Manager*
*Zaneville Credit Union*
*35 High Street*
*Zaneville, Illinois*
*Dear Mr. Eagle:*

*I would like to apply for a loan of $3,500 to be used for prescribed orthodontic work.*

*I am 25, single, and live with my parents, Mr. and Mrs. Joseph P. Worthy, at 562 Elm Street in Zanesville, where they have lived for fifteen years.*

*In the three years since graduating from Normal State, I've been employed as a salesman by Tight Roofing Corp., 13 N. High Street, Zanesville. At present, I earn $18,000 a year. Unfortunately, the company doesn't have a dental insurance program.*

*I have a savings account with Temple Savings (#16534) that now totals $2,000. In addition, I carry a $50,000 Aetna life insurance policy with a cash surrender value of $4,000.*

*My principal financial obligation is my car loan with USAC on a 1983 United Excaliber LTD—I have two months to go on it and the payments are $125 a month. Also, I pay my parents $30 a week board. My credit rating is excellent.*

---

*Thank you for your consideration.*

*Very truly,*
*George J. Worthy*

George had supplied all the necessary information in an easy-to-follow, straightforward manner, and the letter had a sincere feeling. After the credit union's routine check with its credit bureau, George got his loan.

There may be a time when your application for credit is turned down. By law, the lender is required to give you an explanation. There are five reasons for refusing credit:

*Credit Status.* This relates to your file with credit bureaus. The no-no's that will earn you a poor credit status range from bankruptcy to not having established a credit history. "Excessive obligations" is the term used most often.

*Employment status.* The negatives here are inability to verify your job, insufficient time on the job, or an irregular working pattern, such as too many absences.

*Income.* Either your income is too low or it cannot be adequately documented.

*Residency.* You'll be turned down if you haven't lived at one address long enough, or if the lender can't verify the address.

*Other.* This is a catchall that includes such situations as a bad credit file on you, an incomplete application, or insufficient collateral.

In Bob Bottomline's case, the bank turned down his request for a car loan because of "delinquent credit obligations." He found out that the bank's credit bureau was Acme Credit Information Co. and contacted them directly. He was given the specifics, as was his right legally, so he was able to write this letter to the bank with a copy to Acme:

> *Mr. Oscar M. Gotrocks, Manager*
> *Third National Bank*
> *455 Main Street*
> *Oswego, N.Y.*
> *Dear Mr. Gotrocks:*
>
> *This letter concerns my application (#635178) to the Third National Bank for a $7,000 car loan.*
>
> *Enclosed are copies of my June 16, 1985 application and the Third National's letter of June 21, 1985, informing me that the loan was not approved because of "delinquent credit obligations." At that time you advised me that I could get more information about this from Acme Credit Information Co.*
>
> *Acme supplied the reason for my credit problem. Their records showed a 60-day over-due payment to Lacy's Department Store for furniture I had purchased in April.*
>
> *On contacting Lacy's, the store confirmed my explanation that my nonpayment of the bill was due to the damaged condition of the furniture I received, and to the time needed to adjust the matter. Note the enclosed Lacy letter to Acme dated June 30, 1985, which has cleared my credit record.*
>
> *Consequently, Mr. Gotrocks, I would like*

*to reapply for the car loan. Please let me know
if there is anything further that I should do.*

*Sincerely,*
*Robert Bottomline*

cc: *Acme Credit Information Co.*


Bob had provided all the information necessary to clear up the credit problem, not only with Third National, but with the credit bureau (which was required by law to update his file so that his good standing was restored). He also made it easy for the bank to proceed with the loan application by enclosing copies of his correspondence.

Happily, he got the loan and is enjoying his new sports car.

Many people have credit problems because of events beyond their control. Common pitfalls are job loss, illness, and family problems. But most bad risks get in over their heads through plain poor planning.

With the world running on plastic these days, and the outlook being for even more credit in the so-called cashless society of the future, it's easy for people to get overextended. It is vital, when that happens, to take steps to restore your rating and have your file reflect your efforts. That's because a good credit record can be at least as valuable as a good job when it comes to borrowing. What's more, since many employers check applicants' credit files, your very job could depend on the kind of payment profile they find there.

Joe Poorchoice's situation was not all that unusual. He and Laura Highlife had a whirlwind romance and tied the knot in a hurry. By the time Joe discovered Laura's champagne tastes, it was too late. Even though she had a good job that paid top dollar, Laura brought to the marriage a triple-X rather than triple-A credit rating, and extravagant behavior to go with it.

Soon Laura was up to her old tricks, living life in the fast financial lane and putting it all on plastic, Joe's as well as her own. They began charging things they had once paid cash for. As the bills mounted, so did the fights. The first of the month became a nightmare, as they fell farther and farther behind in dealing with dozens of increasingly urgent demands for payment.

When they realized that the ostrich approach wouldn't work and the bills weren't going away, they agreed to get help. Since Laura loved Joe and they wanted eventually to own a home and start a family, she was motivated to mend her ways. They obtained the name of a credit-counseling service in their hometown by writing the National Foundation for Consumer Credit, 1819 H Street, N.W., Washington, D.C. 20006. These two hundred nonprofit organizations across the U.S. are funded by banks, stores, and other lending institutions to offer help free or at a nominal charge because it is in their best interests to help people use credit wisely.

With the aid of a sympathetic credit counselor, the Poorchoices took a clear-eyed look at their cash-flow and credit-crunch problems. They also drew up their first-ever realistic budget. Since they were juggling so many bills, the counselor agreed to consolidate all their debts, arrange for one monthly payment, and inform all the Poorchoices' creditors and collection agencies.

Meanwhile Joe and Laura decided to give plastic a rest and cut down on nonessentials like lengthy long-distance calls, eating out, and luxury vacations.

Here's the letter they wrote confirming their arrangements with the counselor:

*Mr. Leland Thrifty*
*Budget & Credit Counseling Service, Inc.*
*1001 Palmer Avenue*
*Bronxville, N.Y. 10708*
*Dear Mr. Thrifty:*

*Many thanks for all you did to help us organize our financial affairs when it seemed that our only out was bankruptcy.*

*This is to confirm our agreement that you will contact all our creditors. A list of their names and addresses and the amounts owed is attached. With their agreement, we plan to pay back our total indebtedness of $6,520 over the next year in 12 monthly payments, incurring no new debts during that period.*

*As you recommended, we are getting rid of our second car, which will make our other belt-tightening measures less stringent. Since Laura plans to jog to the railroad station, she is giving up her health club membership, a further economy!*

*Thanks to you and the understanding of our creditors, we hope to make a new start come November 1986.*

*Gratefully yours,*
*Joseph Poorchoice*

The Poorchoices were smart to get help when they did. Filing for personal bankruptcy can stay on your credit record up to fourteen years, instead of the seven years for other payment problems.

However, you can start turning your credit report around immediately, as the Poorchoices did. It's worth reestablishing yourself as creditworthy, even if it takes seven years before you're totally in the clear. Fortunately, even one year of "on-time" payments will be considered by lenders as evidence of an improved attitude toward credit management, especially if there is documentation of that change in your file.

There are times when you may want to rewrite your credit history. One is if there is incorrect or incomplete information in your file. Credit bureaus issue an estimated 150 million reports annually and admit to errors in one out of every fifty cases. It's worth a check of your own record to be sure you're not one of the unlucky 2 percent. By law you have the right to be told the nature, substance, and sources of the information collected about you.

The credit agency must reinvestigate inaccurate material on you and, when justified, remove or correct it. Further, it must notify those who have received erroneous information of the change in your favor.

Rewriting their credit history is of particular importance to married, divorced, separated, or widowed women. They may not have complete or accurate credit histories in their own names as opposed to their husbands'. That's a problem, even though the law since 1977 stipulated that creditors reporting information to credit bureaus on joint accounts do so in both spouses' names.

This hurt Prudence Poundfoolish as she tried to obtain credit when she separated from her imprudent husband, Paul. His spendthrift behavior was the main cause of the marital rift. Most of their financial dealings had been conducted in his name, including their growing indebtedness. Since Prudence had moved across the country from her native California when they married three years before, the triple-A credit record she had established in her maiden name was not reflected in their joint file at local credit bureaus.

She contacted the West Coast bureaus that were able to vouch for her earlier creditworthiness as Ms. Prudence Prompt. She called the New England credit bureaus, then wrote them the following letter to set the record straight:

*Ms. Rachel Case*
*Union Credit Data Co.*
*22 Threadneedle Street*
*Boston, MA*
*Dear Ms. Case:*

*As discussed on the phone, the bad credit rating in your files under my married name, Prudence P. Poundfoolish (Mrs. Paul), is the result of delinquent debts contracted by my husband, from whom I am legally separated. Since his fiscal irresponsibility is the key reason for our separation, I wish to have my credit history revised to include evidence of my creditworthiness during the five years prior to my marriage.*

*I have already instructed Golden Credit Bureau of Los Angeles to forward to you the credit record I established under my maiden name, Ms. Prudence Prompt.*

*It is an accurate picture of my responsible financial behavior, which your current file does*

not portray. Please amend your files accord-
ingly. Thank you.

> Sincerely,
> Prudence Prompt
> Poundfoolish

cc: Mr. Nugget, Golden Credit Bureau

Prudence's file was amended and she was able to pass
credit checks by both a potential employer and her bank,
where she had established a new account and gotten a
charge card in her own name.

## Putting It All Together

The secret of success in your communications about
credit is to have all your financial dealings reflect the
triple-A way in which you conduct yourself—your *ability*
to repay, the *assets* you possess, and your positive
*attitude*.

Then, in the actual communications applying for or
dealing with credit, there are four key rules.

*Remember:*

—Be straightforward in providing the facts.
—Keep it brief.
—Show stability and consistency.
—Direct it to the right person.

# CHAPTER SIX

# THE PERSONAL LOAN LETTER
## HOW TO BORROW FROM FRIENDS AND FAMILY

Someone once said, "The shoulders of a borrower are always a little straighter than those of a beggar." But not much. We may dread asking for money or credit from an institution like a bank or finance company as discussed in the preceding chapter. But at least they are in the business of lending money.

There's always a sort of additional, if unspoken, stigma associated with borrowing from a friend or relative. Still and all, there are times when you have no choice. The usual lending institutions simply aren't an option because of the nature of the loan, or perhaps you lack an established credit record.

There can be very legitimate circumstances requiring a personal loan that are recognized and appreciated by the lender as well as by the borrower. For example, a loan may be needed to finance further education that will pay off in the future, and the lender not only has the means but is vitally interested in the career aspirations of the borrower.

Most often, however, asking someone you know for money is a gut-wrenching experience because it means compromising your pride. You may have failed in some way and are caught short or even completely without money. Worse yet, whether the request is granted or not, just asking creates some uncomfortable alternatives. If the request is granted, you now owe your creditor a favor. If it isn't, you are likely to end up mad at the person: "That s.o.b., after all I've done for him!"

Difficult as it is to ask for a personal loan, it's almost as painful to be asked. While the acquaintance, friend, or relative you've approached is silently cursing you for asking for money, he's probably also wondering whether he'll ever get it back. Or he may be agonizing over how to turn you down without losing your friendship.

A good loan request letter can ease the pain at both ends. And, heaven forbid, should you be the victim of an even worse scenario and be unable to repay the loan, the lender with a letter in his possession can at least write it off his taxes as a bad debt. In this chapter we'll deal with letters asking for personal loans, and with corresponding responses.

## Rules of the Game

There are four important principles to remember in writing a personal loan letter.

*1. Even though it's personal, make it business-*

*like.* Money matters are taken very seriously, and you should avoid any misunderstandings about the transaction.

2. *Include a plan for repayment.* Leave no doubt that you intend to see that the lender will get his money back.

3. *Offer to pay interest,* at a mutually agreeable rate. After all, that money could be making money for the lender somewhere else. Psychologically, the interest paid is a small price for the straighter shoulders of a businesslike borrower rather than the bowed ones of a beggar.

4. *Pick your prospect carefully.* Because such a transaction is often emotionally charged, it's likely that you should not involve the person that at first glance seems the closest and most logical. Perhaps, for example, your target should be an affluent old school friend rather than your live-in lover, whose fiscal philosophy is strictly pay-as-you-go. Or, if you have a rich but nosy in-law that you would rather keep out of your financial hair, a more distant relative would be a better bet.

The opening paragraph of your letter should be direct and to the point yet friendly in tone. After all, you are asking for an important favor. But there's no point in beating around the bush. Get to the point—fast! Don't make the person guess what it's all about, with the possibility of misunderstanding and consequent mistrust.

Cover the reason for asking *him.* A little flattery can help. If it's within the family, compliment him on the past support he has given you or other family members. Perhaps you're asking a friend for money for business reasons. Use his business vision and imagination as the reason you "selected" him over all others to ask.

The middle section of the letter should explain the purpose of the loan, including the reasons that led to your need for the money. These can range from dire circumstances, such as a family tragedy, to a happy opportunity. Explain the benefits of making the loan, not only to you the borrower, but also, one hopes, to the lender. Maybe it's the satisfaction of knowing he's helped a family member avoid financial disaster. Or maybe you're offering the opportunity to be helpful in financing a business breakthrough. Whatever the cause, the letter should get the recipient directly involved.

Your repayment proposal should come right after your explanation of the need for the loan. It should be very specific and explain the payment period and the interest rate the loan should carry. Many personal loans are based on an average of the prime interest over the previous twelve months, which should appeal to the lender as well as the borrower as a reasonable business proposition.

But invite his input on how he would like the loan repaid. He might want it paid in a certain way. For example, repayment could relate to his tax status at a particular time or to other financial circumstances. It's another way of involving *him* and demonstrating your consideration.

Incidentally, don't be surprised if your potential benefactor insists on showing your letter to his lawyer. Knowing that he's legally protected may work in your favor; he'll be more amenable to making the loan.

The closing section should explain how you will follow up. Perhaps you'll promise a visit or phone call. If the request is a real long shot—maybe you aren't sure of the lender's finances—you might provide him with an out. This reduces the embarrassment to both parties if you're turned down.

## SOME EXAMPLES

Blood may be thicker than water, but you may feel as if you're wringing that same blood from a stone when you ask a relative for a loan.

Such was the case with Mary Midastouch. Her mother had died of cancer when she was twelve, which left Mary riding herd on her two brothers, ten and eight, and a sister, six. She welcomed the relief from responsibility three years later when her father married a wonderful widow with two young sons of her own. The blended family, strong believers in education, planned to send the six kids to good colleges, even if it meant hard work and skimping by all hands. However, it was agreed that, for any advanced study beyond the undergraduate level, each youngster was on his/her own.

Mary graduated with honors in fine arts from a small liberal arts college. Unable to support herself with her work as a sculptor, she got into the management training program of a home furnishings retailer. There she discovered she had a flair for interior design, plus keen business sense, and advanced rapidly. She pursued her sculpture after hours and on her days off. It soon became clear to Mary that if she was to move in to top management in order to realize her long-term goal of heading her own interior design firm, where sculpture would play an integral role, she needed an M.B.A.

Her firm had a program offering part payment for night-school credits gained while working. However, Mary knew she would need several years to complete her degree that way. Besides, top-level opportunities for women beckoned immediately, and the chain agreed to give her a leave of absence if she could get the degree herself in the minimum time possible.

Because of cutbacks in federal student loan programs, Mary was able to come up with only half the funding she estimated she would need to complete an eighteen-month program at the prestigious Wampus University, attended by both her father and grandfather.

She had two family members to tap for a personal loan. One was her paternal grandfather, conservative old Mark Midastouch, who was vocal in his disapproval of higher education for women. A better bet, Mary concluded, was her widowed maternal grandmother, who had been left quite comfortably off by her husband. This older lady was herself keenly interested in finance but was frustrated by family pressures that had denied her a paid job outside the home when she was younger. She managed her own portfolio and was warmly supportive of her granddaughter's career. Here's the letter that Mary wrote her:

*Dearest Gran:*

*It was wonderful seeing you last week. I always come away from our visits with renewed admiration for my gutsy grandmother—and funnily enough, with strengthened confidence in myself. It's great to feel you're in my corner and to hope that I was lucky enough to have inherited some of the zest for living that makes you so special.*

*Since this is so tough for me (who was it that said it's harder for WASPs to talk about money than sex—and that's hard enough?), I'll*

come right to the point. I need your help—
financial, that is.

As you know, the good news is that I have
a chance to get my M.B.A. But the bad news is
that despite my best efforts, I can only come up
with half the financing.

So I'd like to make you a business proposition. Would you be willing to lend me $500 a
month for the next 18 months? As you know,
Dad and Sheila are paying two college tuitions
for the boys, so they couldn't help even if I
wanted to ask them. Since the loans and grants
I'm getting will take care of tuition, the money
I need is for ongoing living expenses as well as
books and other academic necessities.

Not lending me a lump sum up front
means you can keep your other investments
working as long as possible. I hope you'll think
of this as an investment, too—in your granddaughter's future as a businesswoman—and
that it will prove one of your more gilt-edged
ones! I will pay you back, of course, at the
prevailing prime rate of interest averaged over
the amount and period of the loan.

According to my calculations, when I
rejoin Designs for Living, I should be able to
double my salary within a year and begin paying you back monthly at a rate of 10% of my
take-home pay. That means I could start
repaying at $200 a month as of April 1987 and
raise it to $500 monthly by April 1988.

Please think it over, Gran. If for any reason you feel you can't make the loan, I'm sure
the reasons will be sound and it won't make the

*slightest difference in our relationship. I'll call
you next week for your decision.*

*Incidentally, if you feel you <u>can</u> do it, a
neat young lawyer I'm seeing offered to put my
repayment agreement in writing—for free!
Mark says he's always wanted to meet the
world's greatest grandmother and only hopes
his work will pass the test of those sharp eyes
he's heard so much about!*

> *Dearest love,*
> *Mary*

Mary had done it all right. She came right to the
point without beating around the bush, made the $500
monthly sums seem more manageable than the stark
$9,000 total, gave good business and personal reasons for
the loan, and offered a reasonable repayment plan (carrying a legal freebie that she thought would appeal to
Gran's bargain-hunting instincts).

So it was with happy anticipation that Mary opened
a letter from her grandmother later that week, only to
have her hopes turn to dismay.

*My Very Dear Granddaughter:*

*Thank you for your letter of Tuesday con-
taining such a very well-thought-out proposal
that I lend you the money you need to further
your education.*

*Unfortunately, my dear, I cannot consider
making a loan of such magnitude to you, no
matter how worthy the cause. With the uncer-
tainties of the present economy, I could not*

*live with myself if I felt I was dipping into my limited capital. The income from my modest investments is all that keeps me from being a burden to my children who, as you know, have money worries of their own.*

*If only I could offer to give you the money outright, I would. But since I cannot, I'd feel most uncomfortable that my need for repayment of a loan would be contributing to the already heavy debt with which you will be burdened as you leave graduate school. I deeply regret that this is the case.*

*I so admire your spirit and desire to improve yourself that I can't believe you won't find another way to finance your M.B.A.*

*Meanwhile, since our old family lawyer Elias Tome retired from Crochett, Hidebound and Tome and I'm in the market for a lawyer with fresh ideas to handle my affairs, won't you bring your young man to tea? Call me.*

*With dearest love to the girl I'm sure will still be the first M.B.A. in the Midastouch family,*

> *Your devoted,*
> *Gran*

Adam Earth encountered a similar dilemma when he asked for a loan. The son of self-made millionaire Max "Mineshaft" Earth, Adam was an early ecology buff. As an environmental sciences major at Alternate Lifestyle University, he had worked on a number of government-funded space projects researching photovoltaics (the way to turn sunlight into electricity). He then spent several years with Applied Solar Energy, Inc., experimenting with the use of advanced materials to increase the efficiency and economy of photovoltaic (PV) cells. He had a small lab at home where he did his own experiments.

Eventually he thought he had achieved a breakthrough that would make PV cells cost-efficient for a wide range of consumer applications and decided to go into business for himself to pursue its development. What Adam needed was a backer.

The obvious candidate was his father. But everything Adam did—from his beard and macrobiotic diet to the "No Nukes is Good Nukes" and "Split Wood Not Atoms" bumper stickers on his car—roused his father's ire. Adam dreaded the old argument about his going into the family strip-mining business. It was sure to be revived by any request for financing.

So he decided to approach his college roommate, Seth Thermal, a fellow environmentalist, who had already made his first million supplying communities with installations that converted garbage into energy. Here's the letter Adam wrote him:

*Dear Seth:*

*It was great to see you at our tenth reunion and hear of the success of your garbage-conversion business and your after-hours efforts on the wind farm. Now I'd like to make you an offer I hope you won't want to refuse.*

*As a pioneer in the "trash-into-flash-and-cash" field, how would you like to make your second million participating in what is certain to be the next big breakthrough in the renewa-*

ble energy area? I'd like to borrow $100,000 from you to make this happen.

As you know, I've been working these past years at Applied Solar Energy on the application of advanced materials, including gallium arsenide, to PV cells. In the course of my own experiments, I believe I have quite literally stumbled onto a revolutionary new approach and process that will bring energy generated by PV cells well within the $2 per peak watt range (versus today's $8) that most experts consider essential for widespread consumer applications.

As the attached article from Solar Age notes, this is a development not expected until the 1990s and one which will catapult the PV industry into the billion-dollar category.

I have saved enough money during my last 18 months at ASE to live for the next two years off the payroll. The $100,000 I'd like to borrow from you would go toward the equipment, materials, and legal/business counsel I need to bring my process to the patent and marketable stages.

Best estimates by my production and marketing consultants are for breakeven in two years and profits sufficient for paying you back with mutually agreed-upon interest at the rate of one-third of capital plus interest in 1988, and the remainder in 1989. Unless, of course, you'd rather exchange your loan equity at that point for preferred stock in the PV Pioneer Corporation that I'm in the process of forming. A prospectus will be in the mail to you next week.

*That's where the second million-dollar opportunity comes in! You might want to check the whole thing out with your lawyers and accountants. So, think it over. I'll give you a ring next week to see if my hunch is correct that you'll want to be in on the ground floor of an innovation which could revolutionize the future of the renewable-energy business.*

> *As always,*
> *Adam*

Here, too, Adam had covered all the bases, from flattering references to Seth's personal environmental commitment to evidence of sound business reasons for the loan.

But alas, his timing was against him. Seth wrote back by return mail:

*Dear Adam:*

*I could kick myself. If only I'd had your PV cell proposition a month ago! I've just put every last extra cent (and some I've borrowed) into a very promising venture for the cost-efficient conversion of crabgrass into gasohol.*

*But do not despair. When I get your prospectus, I'll forward it, along with your letter and a recommendation from me, to the Energy Foundation. It was established to provide grants and seed money for likely ventures in energy conservation.*

*Yours sounds like a shoo-in—and you don't have to pay the foundation back, merely*

*agree to encourage similar activity by others if
yours is successful. That should provide a boost
to your bottom line.*

*Stella and I would love to see you at Four
Winds Farm. And keep me posted on the PV
project.*

> *All the best,*
> *Seth*

## Putting It All Together

If you can't work through the regular lending institutions and *have* to get a personal loan—then a letter is a
must. It's the first step in a very serious matter.

### Remember:

—Make it businesslike and easy to follow.
—Include a specific repayment proposal that
  doesn't penalize the lender for investing in you.
  Be guided by the lending institutions' current
  rates.
—Above all, choose the right person—not necessarily the closest!
(—And, remember, saying no to a friend or relative
  is just as hard as asking for a loan. Be prompt,
  honest, and as supportive as possible.)

# CHAPTER SEVEN

# THE COMPLAINT LETTER
## HOW TO GET SATISFACTION

The best kind of complaint letter is the one you never have to write. That's because you exercise your responsibilities as a careful shopper up front.

As a responsible consumer, you understand all the fine print before signing anything; get every verbal agreement in writing; inspect all products or repair work before paying; and heed the good advice about a bargain—that if it sounds too good to be true, it probably is! You also try, when things do go on the fritz, to get satisfaction promptly in person or by phone.

Even so, in this increasingly complex computerized world, there comes a time when it is necessary to take pen in hand to protest some indignity perpetrated against you by a merchant, manufacturer, or supplier of services—or sometimes even by a neighbor or friend.

A good complaint letter can work in a wide range of situations, from serious ones like getting stuck with an outsized phone bill for calls you never made or a newly installed roof that leaks, to minor ones like a faulty toaster or the neighbor's dog that never stops barking. While the contents may differ, the basic principles remain the same. When addressed to reasonable people—and most people really are reasonable—a good complaint letter will spur action. Studies show that half of all people who write letters expressing their grievances get satisfaction. What about the other half? If everyone followed these simple guidelines, their batting average would be higher!

## Rules of the Game

The following seven points apply to almost all complaint letters:

1. *Organize your strategy and documentation up front.* Before making a move, think through the problem and possible solutions. Does the situation really warrant a letter? If so, develop a clear, well-documented appeal. Include all the pertinent details: dates, locations, names of people, model numbers, receipts, warranties, etc. This shows you are buttoned up and helps the respondent deal with the problem. Always make copies of your letters and attachments. Never, repeat, *never*, send the originals.

2. *Strive for a balanced tone.* Even if the temptation to blast the offending party is great, don't do it! Insults only put the recipient on the defensive. All that energy could be put to better use. Be polite, but firm. Avoid sarcasm and smart remarks. If you are bucking established policy, don't waste time arguing with the rule book. Instead, show that your case is unique and

deserves special attention. Enlist the recipient's aid in seeking a solution.

3. *Keep it brief and to the point.* Short is sweet. Include only the essentials.

4. *Neatness pays off.* Your letter should be businesslike and in almost all cases neatly typed. If you must write by hand, be sure it's legible. Letters that are tough to decipher get short shrift.

5. *Make clear what specific action you want.* Suggest a deadline so your problem isn't put on the back burner.

6. *Indicate that copies of your complaint letter are going to third parties*—the Better Business Bureau, a government department of consumer affairs, even the advertising media (if the product or service was bought through their ads).

7. *Personalize.* Elicit sympathy by positioning yourself as vulnerable or the victim of circumstances.

## Who Should Get the Letter?

There are different points of view on this. With corporations or government agencies, I favor going to the top, where the power is, providing the issue is important. Certainly it's indicated if you haven't been able to get satisfaction lower down. Don't bother a CEO with a two-dollar beef—it isn't worth your time and certainly not his. But if your complaint is valid and the company is concerned about its public image (and most are these days), write to a specific person in the upper echelons.

You can get the name, title, and address from your local library. Two good sources are the *Thomas Register*, a listing of who makes what, and *Standard & Poor's Register of Corporations, Directors and Executives*. Or call the company and ask the switchboard operator for the name of the president or executive vice-president.

The CEO probably won't read your letter unless it involves a critical problem that he's trying to evaluate at the time. But it certainly will be directed to the proper people for action. Once it has passed through the CEO's office, it will have priority. If an outside agency has been copied, its priority will be even greater.

If the problem is a minor one, such as difficulty with a recipe on the product's package, you'll get satisfaction from the home economist or the company's consumer affairs department.

### SOME EXAMPLES

The first call came at 3:00 in the morning. The next ones at 3:22, 4:12, and then at odd intervals. By 7:00 A.M., the damage had been done. Steve Straight and his wife, Nancy, didn't get a wink of sleep all night.

The calls were always the same—a voice in the night asking for the time. At first, Steve and Nancy patiently explained that the party had the wrong number. But after a while they weren't so polite and began asking themselves if someone was playing a prank and, if so, why.

As soon as Steve left for work, Nancy was on the phone to the telephone company's service department to complain. The service representative listened, then said she would investigate and report back. But she didn't.

That day and the next night, it was more of the same. Steve finally took the phone off the hook, accompanied by some unprintable expletives about phones in general and the company in particular. The next day Nancy tracked down the service rep again and demanded an explanation. Their report, which infuriated Nancy, was that their investigation showed there *really was* a problem. But nobody seemed to know what to do about it.

So Nancy got the department supervisor on the line. A day later an explanation finally surfaced. Apparently the Straights' number was similar to one people call to get the time, and there was a short circuit. Now the company offered a solution! The Straights could have their number changed without charge. But who needs that? asked Nancy. She'd have to notify everyone—friends, relatives, business people, and charge accounts. The next directory wouldn't be out for a year.

That's when they fired off a letter of complaint to the president of the company, with a copy to the state Public Service Commission. Here it is:

*Mr. Ralph K. Longlines, President*
*Acme Phone Company*
*12 Main Street*
*Elm Rapids, Ohio*
*Dear Mr. Longlines:*

*My family has, until recently, been pleased with the phone service provided by Acme. In fact, on one occasion when we had a minor fire, your operator volunteered to call all the emergency services that were needed. Needless to say, we were grateful.*

*However, we now have a serious problem*

*that your people are having trouble solving. We
are getting phone calls at all hours of the day
and night asking for the time. On the attached
you will see a chronological account of Acme
personnel involved, and action taken so far.*

*This has been going on for days now, and
the only suggestion offered involved our changing our phone number. Isn't there a better
way?*

*We'll be grateful for anything you can do.*

*Sincerely,
Stephen P. Straight*

*cc: Public Service Commission*

It worked! Steve had gone to the top, but only after
demonstrating that he had tried at other levels and failed.
His tone was polite and reasonable. And he copied the
right third party, the PSC, which regulates the phone
industry.

Mr. Longlines assigned a senior service executive to
the case, who reported progress daily to the Straights—
and to Mr. Longlines. An intercept, screening out the time
calls, was put on their incoming calls until the problem
was solved.

Judy Hardluck was a victim of double billing by a
furniture store.

She really had scraped to come up with the $750 for
the "bargain" three-piece bedroom suite she bought at
Wobbly Furniture, not the most reputable dealer in San
Diego. After picking out what she wanted, Judy had
withdrawn the money from her savings account, gotten a

money order from the post office, and completed the transaction.

Disaster struck three weeks later when a fire swept through Judy's apartment building, wrecking much of it, including her new furniture. That was bad enough, but when a bill for the suite came from Wobbly, she really cried. Judy had no record of having paid the $750; the receipt had been lost in the fire! Appeals to the store got her nowhere; Wobbly wanted their money. They threatened to put the matter in the hands of a collection agency, which would have been bad for Judy's credit rating, so she wrote this letter:

*Mr. Nathan Sharpy, President*
*Wobbly Furniture, Inc.*
*Shabby Street*
*San Diego, California*
*Dear Mr. Sharpy:*

*As you know, due to a fire in my apartment, I have been unable to find a record of having paid $750 by money order for the furniture I bought from you four weeks ago. Your people don't seem to maintain very good records. This is a real hardship case, as I explained, because the furniture has been destroyed.*

*By copy of this letter I am asking you not to put this matter in the hands of your collection agency. I suggest a further review of your accounts. At the same time, I will see if there is some way I can re-create my record.*

*Because of the hardship nature of this situation and Wobbly's lack of compassion, I am sending a copy of this letter to the Better Business Bureau.*

*Sincerely,*
*Judy Hardluck*

*cc: Better Business Bureau*

Judy's straightforward letter, and her remembering to copy the Better Business Bureau, worked and the firm backed off. This gave Judy time to come up with a copy of the money order through the post office, and the matter was resolved.

When Wendy Wonderful got engaged to Mark Marvelous, her friends gave the couple a kitchen shower. One gift was an E-Z Daisy electric can opener, designed to grip the can as it is opened, and then release it while a magnetic device holds the lid.

No sooner had Wendy installed it than her troubles began. The grip released the cans too soon, dumping them and their contents onto the floor and Wendy. Neither the instruction booklet nor her handy fiancé could shed any light on the problem. A big toe damaged by a sixteen-ounce can of baked beans was the last straw.

After an embarrassing call to the donor to find out where it had been purchased, Wendy took the can opener back to the discount store, only to discover that the ten-day period for returns had elapsed. A surly manager turned a deaf ear to her problem and told her to contact the local E-Z Daisy distributor.

But the distributor refused to take any responsibility without a sales receipt, even though Wendy explained the appliance had been a gift. He told her to write the manufacturer. So here is the letter that Wendy, by now thoroughly fed up, wrote:

*Mr. Matthew Mismanagement, President*
*E-Z Daisy Appliance Co.*
*One Daisy Way*
*Mechanicsville, N.Y.*
*Dear Mr. Mismanagement:*

    *I recently received as a bridal shower gift an E-Z Daisy can opener, Model # 567, Serial # 1001. It was purchased on May 25, 1985 at Crazy Teddy's Discount Store, Main St., Center City, N.Y.*

    *Unfortunately, though we've followed the operating instructions, the opener's grip is defective and drops the cans midway through the opening process.*

    *I took the appliance back to Crazy Teddy's, and then, at their advice, to the local E-Z Daisy distributor, Edgar Unhelpful. I had the warranty, but Mr. Unhelpful refused to repair or replace it without a receipt. Because it was a gift, I didn't have one.*

    *Please advise me how I can get my can opener repaired or replaced. I've long been a fan of E-Z Daisy Appliances. As a bride-to-be planning to furnish a new home, I'd be very disappointed if this unfortunate experience with one of your products is typical.*

    *Your advertising on WTNT, our local radio station, stresses E-Z Daisy's quality and service. The friend who gave me the can opener wants to contact their* Call for Action *consumer program to complain. But I've asked her to hold off because I feel sure you will want to help us resolve the problem as soon as possible.*

*Looking forward to hearing from you.*

*Sincerely,*
*Wendy Wonderful*

Wendy had followed the rules to a T. She went to the top, including all the facts in a courteous but firm manner. In addition, there was the promise of future business from her as well as the subtle threat of bad publicity if she didn't get satisfaction.

Three days later, Mr. Mismanagement called and arranged for the delivery of a new can opener. In addition, an E-Z Daisy consumer representative followed up several weeks later to make sure all was well. Nice going, Wendy!

Here's another trying situation a lot of people face these days:

Young, upwardly mobile Abby and Al Affluent were accustomed to the stacks of catalogs, fund-raising appeals, and once-in-a-lifetime bargain product offers that arrived at their art-filled town house by mail each week. In fact, they enjoyed leafing through the luxury items and letting their fingers do the walking through the upscale outdoor gear from Abergrabber & Snatch.

But they drew the line when they began to get computerized letters starting like this: "Dear Owner of a 1985 Ford Thunderbird: Is your new luxury car fully protected against vandalism and theft?" Or: "As a collector of antiques and fine art, you are a prime target for robbery! Therefore you shouldn't waste a minute before calling us for a free demonstration of our SAFE-T antiburglary system." Adult entertainment offers for X-rated videocassettes addressed to Al infuriated Abby (she threw away one catalog of "sexual aids" from Eros Unlimited before Al could see it).

Nervous about criminals' ability to get the same mailing lists, and sick of porn offers, the Affluents decided to turn off the mail at the source. But this was easier said than done because they owned every credit card available; they subscribed to dozens of magazines; and they ordered from numerous catalogs. They knew their names were on lists widely rented out by list brokers. But they were determined to cut down the avalanche of mail.

Here is the form letter they put together and sent to each of the forty-five direct mail-order companies they wished to cancel:

*Dear ———:*

*A man's home is no longer his castle when his privacy is invaded by unsolicitated mailings such as yours. The possibility that the computerized list you are using could fall into unscrupulous hands prompts us to request that you remove our names and address from your mailing list for any and all purposes, including further promotion of your products. We are sure you can understand our concern.*

*As evidence of our determination to reassert our right to privacy, and as proof that we will consider failure to follow our instructions a breach of business ethics, we are sending a copy of this letter to the County Office of Consumer Complaints.*

*However, we feel sure that, as a company in business in good faith and interested in customer satisfaction, you will comply promptly with our request.*

*Sincerely,*
*Albert Affluent*

*cc: County Office of Consumer Complaints*

The Affluents received courteous letters from most of the companies they contacted and, slowly but surely, they watched the volume of junk mail abate. Their letter was successful because it was brief, enlisted sympathy and cooperation, and added an incentive by bringing in the County Office of Consumer Complaints.

A few days later when they were discussing the experience with friends, the Affluents discovered there was an easier way. So sensitive is the direct mail industry to its image for ethical conduct and good taste that a letter to the Direct Marketing Association, 6 East 43rd Street, New York, N.Y. 10017, asking for its Mail Preference Form, would have done the trick. On receipt of the completed form, the organization circulates it to the several hundred list brokers, computerized mail, and direct-response companies, requesting removal of your name and address.

While these examples have dealt with product and service problems, the same techniques work for personal ones, closer to home. Robert Frost's neighbor may have been right when he wrote, "Good fences make good neighbors." But fences were no help to Sam and Serena

Suburban and their next-door neighbors, the Humanes, who had recently acquired a black Labrador pup. Not only did the aptly named Satan whimper, whine, and bark whenever the Humanes left him shut in the house, but the moment he was let into the yard, he sought ways to escape to a wider world. If a gate was left open, he was off like a shot for the greener pastures of lawns, gardens, and homes up and down the street. There he put to use his natural talents for digging in flower beds, terrifying cats, retrieving and carrying home found objects from shoes to the Sunday roast, and relieving himself on any attractive surface, including whitewall tires. Numerous complaints by neighbors plus several angry trips to return him to the Humanes had no effect.

Since the Suburbans were next door, they were the most frequent targets of Satan's sorties. Serena's first effort to deal with the problem directly was a diffident exchange over the backyard fence with Harriet. It resulted in a helpless shrug and words to the effect that "He's a devil, but he's so cute," along with a vague promise to try to keep the gate shut.

Things improved for a while, but Satan was not to be stymied. He went underground, digging a hole under the fence between the two houses. One day Satan went too far. He chewed up the legs of the Suburbans' brand-new lawn furniture and deposited the vinyl cushions all over the lawn and in the pool.

The Surburbans were furious, and Sam was ready to go after Satan with his shotgun. But Serena's cool head prevailed as she reminded him that they'd have to live side by side with the Humanes, Satan or no. She also pointed out that the rest of the neighborhood would be grateful if the Suburbans put their mutual grievances in writing. The next day the Surburbans and three other neighbors got together and drafted the following letter:

*Dear Harriet and Hal:*

*There's an hold Hindu proverb, "A dog is a lion in his own lane." Well, this letter is an urgent request for you to take measures to keep your particular lion in his own lane—your property. Unfortunately we are not alone; the entire neighborhood is up in arms.*

*If you can't or won't take steps to protect the property, pets, and peace of mind of the rest of us from Satan, several neighbors plan to appeal to the authorities. On the basis of our long friendship, we'd hate to see that happen.*

*Just so you don't think we're overreacting or are unsympathetic to animals, let us briefly list our grievances to date:*

*3 flower beds dug up*
*4 items of footwear missing*
*1 leg of lamb, dragged from the barbecue and rendered inedible*
*2 holes under the fence*
*1 set of lawn furniture mauled, pillows grass-stained and soaked*
*1 already neurotic cat rendered (forgive us) catatonic*

*The purpose of this letter isn't to request damages, but to prevent further ones. In fact, we'd advocate putting any sums that might fairly be considered restitution toward an obedience training course for Satan.*

*We've checked and there's an excellent one on Willow Avenue. The phone number is 868-4400. We'd suggest calling today; we can't*

*vouch for the continued patience of some of
our mutual neighbors.*

    *Looking forward to the day when Satan is
still cute, but no longer a devil!*

                *Your good friends (and deter-
mined to remain so, Satan
notwithstanding),
Serena and Sam*

Sure enough, the letter produced the desired effect.
The fact that it was sympathetic, well documented, and
humorous and that it offered the Humanes a face-saving
solution (as well as a none-too-subtle threat of neighborhood action) all helped.

Satan graduated from obedience school with honors
and has become a veritable role model of good manners
instead of the neighborhood nuisance. So even this dog's
tale had a happy ending!

## Putting It All Together

The message to all those afflicted with the hassles of
modern-day living is this: When your grievances get to
you, don't waste time in useless verbal arguments. Put
your request for restitution in the form of a letter.

*Remember:*

—Organize your complaints, giving specifics and
    attaching copies of documentation.

—Be polite, but firm. Resist the impulse to let off steam.

—Keep it brief, businesslike, and neat.

—Give a reasonable deadline for action.

—Enlist the clout of an appropriate third party wherever possible.

—Suggest a course of action leading to an acceptable solution.

—Keep copies of all correspondence.

# CHAPTER EIGHT

# THE CLAIM LETTER
## WHEN THE COMPLAINT LETTER ISN'T ENOUGH

Perhaps the complaint letter you wrote (see Chapter 7) didn't work. Or maybe you've found yourself in a situation that requires a stronger, more forceful letter. Perhaps there is a significant sum of money involved, but not enough to warrant hiring a lawyer. It's at this point that you want to *claim* what is due you. You are ready to take action involving the intervention of a third party to settle the matter and help you collect your due.

Now is the time to call on the "threat" letter. The keynote initially (as in the complaint letter) should be persuasion urging compliance, rather than outright threats. If that fails, then use mounting degrees of pressure in pressing your claim, depending on the specific situation and the agency you have selected to help you get action.

Perhaps your old friend hasn't repaid that loan, even after a dozen phone reminders. Or your former landlord won't refund your security deposit though you fulfilled all the requirements when you moved. Or you can't get satisfaction on a car that turned out to be a lemon. There is a wide range of situations that necessitate claim letters. You resort to a letter or letters because you want to include detailed information. And you certainly want to have a written record in case further action is needed. When all else has failed and you're not sure how to proceed on your own, you'll want to enlist the services of a crack lawyer. And then you'll find the written record your letters provide absolutely invaluable.

The minimum amount of pressure is exerted by the complaint letter discussed in the last chapter. It doesn't threaten per se, though copying a third party is an implied threat. That type of letter to a nonadversary serves as a reminder or uses logic to urge the recipient to react. It treats the matter as a possible oversight. Further pressure is exerted by strong appeals to reason and fairness. For example, "If the situation were reversed and you . . ."

But now heavy-duty persuasion is required as you do not just refer to a third party but introduce the specific threat of their intervention. You could be resorting to the help of a consumer agency or trade association, requesting arbitration via the Better Business Bureau, or taking the offender to small-claims court. In any case, earlier efforts weren't successful and you're bringing up your big guns. You have thought it through carefully, and this is your last resort.

## Rules of the Game

Most of the guidelines for the claim letter are similar to those for the complaint letter. However, some aspects become much more important. The first one is critical.

1. *Be very careful not to claim anything that is not really due you.* Don't threaten legal action if you don't mean it. Copies of letters with untruths or exaggerations to third parties that are meant to impress the primary recipient can end up being very damaging. They could lead to charges of fraud, extortion, or blackmail.

2. *Focus on the basic issue.* Explain clearly what is wrong and how it can be righted. Don't obscure your points with extraneous information; merely document your basic points. Keep it brief.

3. *Act promptly,* or you could be defeated by the statute of limitations. These vary by state and can be as little as a year for some types of legal action.

4. *The tone should be firm, courteous, and business like,* not frivolous. Avoid sarcasm because it could be misunderstood.

SOME EXAMPLES

In the past, *caveat emptor* (buyer beware) was the consumer's best bet in avoiding being fleeced. But the era of the educated activist shopper has brought with it agencies to which dissatisfied customers can turn. They can be found under "Consumer Protection" or "Consumer

Action" in the city, county, or state government listings in your phone book.

Take the case of the Strivers and the High Volt Gas and Electric Co. Mary and John Striver simply couldn't get the meter reader to come at a time when someone would be home to let him in. Instead, he came between 8:30 and 9:00 A.M., when John had left for work and Mary was taking their two young kids to school.

This resulted in notes on the Strivers' town house door saying that High Volt had tried to read the meter and they would have to estimate the actual usage. Inevitably, the estimated bill was much higher than the actual consumption. Numerous phone calls and one letter to High Volt to set up a different time for the meter reader to visit their house didn't work. After three months of inflated estimated bills, the Shrivers were fed up. This was the letter that Mary wrote:

> *Mr. Alex C. Starchy, President*
> *High Volt Gas and Electric Co.*
> *Utility Plaza*
> *South Chicago, Ill.*
> *Dear Mr. Starchy:*
>
> *I am referring this matter to you because my repeated phone calls and a letter (copy attached) to your Operations Department have not gotten results. We're trying to solve a problem that began three months ago when my family moved into our town house at 35 Lakeside Dr., South Chicago.*
>
> *That was when the last actual electric meter reading was made. Since then the readings have been estimated because your meter*

*reader has continued to come between 8:30 and 9:00 A.M., when no one is at home to admit him. In my many calls to your Operations Department, I've explained that my husband was at work and I was taking our children to school at that time. Virtually any other hour of the day would find someone home.*

*In checking the utility bills, based on meter readings, of two neighbors in identical town houses, I find our estimated bills are approximately 20% higher than theirs. According to my estimates, we have made High Volt an interest-free loan of approximately $200. This is unacceptable.*

*Though we have not contacted them previously, we are fully prepared to refer the problem to the local Consumer Action Committee for solution.*

> *Very truly yours,*
> *Mary Striver*

Would you believe that two days after sending her letter Mary had a call from Mr. Starchy's office asking what time of day would be most convenient for having the meter read? Also, they advised her that a $200 credit would be applied to the Striver account.

Mary's letter had been straightforward, to the point, and effective. Her threat to resort to the local Consumer Action Committee for help did the trick.

Trade associations of auto dealers, home builders, and other types of businesses are another source of support for buyers who've been burned. They will investigate and, if necessary, take action on consumer complaints. Results are usually quick because business people want to avoid censure by their peers.

All too common these days is the situation where someone is unjustly accused of nonpayment of a bill. That's because so much accounting is computerized and common sense and compassion play very small roles.

So the Grasper Brothers' bill of $133 was a complete surprise to Joyce and Tom Jackson. Sure, they had a charge account with Grasper Brothers, as did just about everybody in Akron. But they hadn't bought anything in months. With Joyce six months pregnant, they had been on a real economy kick—saving for the new arrival, their first. They certainly wouldn't have bought a music stand! Neither played a musical instrument.

Repeated phone calls to the Grasper business office only resulted in more checks of the computer and finally a stream of dunning letters. Normally, Joyce took care of the household accounts. But she became so unnerved over this that Tom stepped in.

He went to work and prepared this letter:


*Mr. George Grasper, Chairman*
*Grasper Brothers, Inc.*
*Scenic Mall*
*Akron, Ohio*
*Dear Mr. Grasper:*

   *I am appealing to you for help in stopping the flow of dunning letters from your accounting department regarding the erroneous idea that my wife and I purchased a music stand from Grasper Brothers. Note the attached file* _of correspondence, most of it computer generated, spanning a three-month period._

_Attached are copies of our letters that were never satisfactorily answered. They note that we do not even own a musical instrument and consequently would never have bought a $133 music stand. We have yet to see the purchase slip for that sale. We believe there was a computer error and we are being harassed._

_Our patience is at an end, and we are prepared to take this matter to the National Retail Merchants Association for investigation and action.._

> _Very truly yours,_
> _Thomas H. Jackson_

_cc: NRMA_

Tom's well-documented letter and the possibility of the matter being dealt with by his fellow retailers made George Grasper look into the matter quickly. No purchase slip could be found. (Months later they found out the computer had misidentified one digit in the Jacksons' charge number.)

The dunning letters stopped immediately, and the Jacksons got a personal letter of apology from Mr. Grasper along with a small gift from the store.

Beyond their role in monitoring consumer complaints and exerting pressure on firms guilty of sharp or shoddy practices, the Better Business Bureaus offer an arbitration service to handle consumer-business disputes.

Take the case of the Scotts and the problem with their new car—a problem that seemed to go on forever.

The last straw was when they were visiting friends two hundred miles from home, and for the ninth time in eight months the car, a 1984 Standard, wouldn't start. They had it towed to the nearest garage ($45) and were told it would be repaired the next day with a new starter. Then came the problem of finding a new starter.

The Scotts stayed with their friends for two extra days while the search for a starter continued. On the third day they called the dealer who had sold them the car and told him they wanted nothing more to do with it and were returning it to him as soon as they could. That time came two weeks later, after they had made the round trip to and from home in a rental car ($325) to pick up their car. The garage told Phil that the car had a permanent alignment problem, which meant that the new starter wouldn't last any longer than the previous ones.

So Phil went to work to have the car replaced. He talked to his dealer and the manufacturer's zone manager and followed up with complaint letters to both. But a month passed and nothing seemed to be happening. Phil began to entertain fantasies of imitating a similar situation he had seen on TV, where a guy who couldn't get his car replaced parked it in front of the dealership with a sign that said, "This lemon was purchased at Malo Brothers."

Instead, he contacted the Better Business Bureau to see if they could help. The bureau listened to his story and said they would be willing to set up an arbitration hearing with the manufacturer. With this as a fallback, Phil decided to make one last effort with this letter to the dealer and with copies to the zone manager and the Better Business Bureau. Note that Phil is using his friendship with the dealer and reference to another new-car order as leverage, along with the threat of BBB intervention.

Mr. William G. Walden, Pres.
Walden Motors
Needham, MA
Dear Bill:

As you know, I have on order with your dealership a 1985 four-door Pegasus, fully equipped at the $13,860 price you quoted. This purchase is a step up from the 1984 Standard model that is under negotiation for replacement with your zone office and the Better Business Bureau.

That order is also contingent on the zone office's paying the $460 starter replacement charge, the $45 towing charge, and the $325 rental-car charge that we incurred as a result of the car's breaking down in Scarsdale. Correspondence is attached.

Alice and I appreciate very much your efforts, Bill, in resolving this, though we understand that your zone people have the final say. We hope that our buying the Pegasus will illustrate our good faith in Walden Motors, as well as in Consolidated Cars. As you know, we have been driving them for more than twenty years and would hate to find it necessary to press our case through the Better Business Bureau.

Cordially,
Phil Scott

cc: Mr. Handson, Zone Manager
Better Business Bureau

Within days the Scotts heard from the Consolidated

zone office that their 1984 Standard would be credited at the full 1984 list price and that the company would also pay all the other costs incurred.

There were two forces at work here: pressure from the dealer who wanted to keep a customer happy, and the threat of Better Business Bureau intervention. But Phil's carrot-and-stick approach was the real secret to success. Plus, he kept his cool.

Where small amounts of money are at stake (the maximum amount varies from state to state, mainly in the $500–$1,000 range), you should consider resorting to small-claims court.

Small-claims courts exist in almost every state for the "little guy" to settle non-criminal disputes involving specific damages. They handle cases that aren't worth referring to higher courts because of time and costs. Expenses are kept down by discouraging the use of attorneys to represent the parties and by eliminating much of the paper work that would be required in a higher court. Usually the hearing is scheduled for a few weeks after the claim is filed, and the case is generally dealt with in only a few minutes. Many cases are settled by the parties involved even before a final decision from the judge or arbitrator.

What's more, a recent study shows that nearly half of the defendants don't show up for trial, so you win by default. The study also shows that in 72 percent of the cases where both sides appeared in court, the plaintiff (you) won.

The kind of case most often handled in small-claims court deals with consumer protection, unpaid bills, and recovery of money or property or damages, particularly those relating to auto accidents.

The procedure for dealing with the small-claims court is easy. It involves two letters.

Your first step after the damage is done is to telephone or visit the person who can solve your problem. If it's a dry cleaner, speak to the owner. If it's a manufacturer, speak to the manager or head of customer service. Set a deadline for settlement.

If the date passes without receiving satisfaction, write the person, restating your case and informing him of your intention to go to small-claims court. Make it brief; no judge will want to deal with a ten-page document. Make sure you have the address and legal name of the company correct. It can only be sued in its legal name.

If you get no reply, write a second letter, which should be extremely brief and pointed. Attach a copy of your first letter and send it by registered mail. Keep the receipt and copies of all correspondence. You now have the documentation you need to go to small-claims court.

You prepare a simple statement of the problem and your claim on a form supplied by the court. This includes your name, whom you are suing and why, and the amount you want in damages. (There is a nominal filing fee, usually five dollars.) If you've waited for over a year to file, you may be too late because of the statute of limitations. Ask what applies in your state. Establishing the amount you wish to sue for is important. Go for as much as you can justify, remembering the dollar limit for your state.

The court clerk will suggest a court date that should be convenient for you and allow enough time to serve the defendant. The court sends a summons to the offender. Then, if the matter is not settled out of court, an informal hearing is held with an arbitrator or judge.

It's a good idea to visit a small-claims court and

watch the proceedings before preparing your case. Have
your evidence in a form that is easy to follow.

That's just what Helen Hospitality did. At one of her
convivial dinner parties, a guest spilled a cup of espresso
on her valuable Oriental rug. She hired Quality Carpet
Cleaners to come clean the rug, stressing its antique and
fragile condition. The shampooing removed the stain all
right, but it also removed much of the glowing color and
left the surface roughened and ruined.

When Helen complained to Quality's owner and
requested money to replace the rug, he not only refused
to take responsibility but suggested that the rug had been
in poor condition beforehand.

Fortunately, Helen had recently had an appraisal of
her antiques, accompanied by color photos of each item.
Fuming, she wrote this letter:

> *Mr. Alan Outright*
> *Quality Carpet Cleaners*
> *4 Crooked Lane*
> *Allentown, PA*
> *Dear Mr. Outright:*
>
> *This is to repeat my request, made in
> person to you this morning, that you reimburse
> me for the Oriental rug that was ruined by
> your employee, Jim Careless, when he
> shampooed it last Tuesday.*
>
> *As you can see from the attached, the rug
> was recently valued at $950.*
>
> *As to your assertion that the rug was in
> poor condition beforehand, I enclose a color
> photo taken last month that shows it was not.*

*My dinner guests will attest to its original
condition before the shampooing.*

*If I do not receive satisfaction by Friday
of next week, I intend to pursue the matter in
small-claims court.*

*Sincerely yours,
Helen Hospitality*

Sure enough, Outright opted to hang tough, so Helen
fired off this brief missive:

*Dear Mr. Outright:*

*Since you have not replied to my letter
(attached) regarding my claim for $950 to
replace the Oriental rug ruined by your
employee, I plan to take the case immediately
to small-claims court for settlement.*

*Sincerely yours,
Helen Hospitality*

Helen had already visited the court, filed her claim,
and lined up her witnesses, when Outright capitulated
and paid her in full. The threat, accompanied by solid
evidence, worked.

## Putting It All Together

The claim or threat letter can work very well for

you, getting action in situations where there's been no response to complaint letters.

### *Remember:*

—Be absolutely honest with the claim you make. Don't bluff or exaggerate. Don't threaten any action you're not prepared to take.

—Target on the basic issue and what you perceive to be the solution—as briefly as possible.

—If your problem can't be settled by cash payment or if the amount exceeds your state's small-claims court limitation, use the threat of third-party action for reinforcement. Consumer action agencies, trade associations, and arbitration by the Better Business Bureau are all options that get results.

—For claims or damages in the under-$1,000 range, don't hesitate to resort to small-claims court, or to the threat of same. You can handle your own case, and action is generally swift.

# CHAPTER NINE

# THE LETTER OF RECOMMENDATION
## HOW TO WRITE AN EFFECTIVE REFERENCE

Remember the old saying, "If you want it done right, do it yourself"? Well, it's true. And it's especially true when it comes to a letter of recommendation—for *you*. After all, who knows you better than you? Who else knows which of your qualities best suit you for a prospective job, a school, or a club membership? Answer: Nobody.

So, if the people you've chosen to ask for letters of recommendation don't mention it first (and they usually do), ask them if it would be all right to write at least a first draft of the letter yourself. This is really the most practical way. Why? Because you're making it easier for them to help you by supplying information like dates and accomplishments that they would have to find out anyway—from you. By helping make it happen, you know not only that it will get done, but probably sooner than it would without your input. Remember, they can always edit the draft you give them, so no one will feel you're forcing their hand. A good opener: "If it'll save you the trouble, I'll rough out a draft and send it over."

## Rules of the Game

Regardless of who writes a letter of recommendation, certain rules apply.

1. *Learn as much as you can about the position or association sought* so that you can accurately assess the candidate's ability to qualify.

2. *Tailor the length of your letter to the situation.* For example, if you are seconding someone for club membership, your letter will be shorter than the one proposing him.

3. *Include details of minor or personal qualifications* that are relevant. Here is the type of information that must be provided to the society, business firm, club, university, or organization the applicant wants to join:

—The applicant's name and what he does.
—The relationship you have (or had) with the applicant. Were you his supervisor, classmate, friend, neighbor, banker? When, where, and how close was the association? Details lend credibility.
—An evaluation of the individual's general abilities and, if possible, specific qualifications.
—An offer to provide additional information by letter, phone call, or over lunch.

4. *Make the tone sincere, but friendly.* This puts the writer on a peer-to-peer basis with the recipient. Be careful not to overdo the flattery. A balanced appraisal connotes good judgment. Speaking of credibility, inclusion of both strong *and* *weaker* points can be very effective. Acknowledging weaknesses, if any, can be disarming and even a little intriguing.

SOME EXAMPLES

Letters of recommendation for jobs range broadly in preparation, depending not only on the situation involved but on the degree of familiarity between the applicant and the letter writer. Certain routine situations, such as financial applications, need little special preparation. Conversely, others, though, require a great deal of care, as, for example, when the person giving the reference is a business colleague of the person he's recommending. The applicant's success could have a bearing—good or bad—on the judgment record of the recommender. Think about that!

While this letter is on the letterhead of George Turboflow, it was drafted by Mabel Gogetter, who is applying for a sales manager's job:

*Mr. Rodney W. Sparkplug, President*
*Marty Motors*
*12 High Street*
*Albany, N.Y.*
*Dear Mr. Sparkplug:*

*It is a privilege and pleasure for me to*

recommend Mabel Gogetter for the position of sales manager with Marty Motors.

Mabel was in my sales group at Zenith, the Buffalo Buick dealership, for three years. During that time she was consistently among the top performers in our sales organization. In 1982, she placed tenth among all Buick sales people in New York State.

In addition to her selling ability, Mabel has leadership qualities, as exemplified by her service in the Navy. There, as a lieutenant JG, she was in charge of twenty-five people, most of them men.

We all regret that Mabel, who is as delightful personally as she is able professionally, has chosen to leave Buffalo. But I feel confident that she would be an enormous asset to Marty Motors, as well as a pleasure to work with.

Very truly yours,
George Turboflow
President, Zenith Buick

Note: Mabel was aware that Mr. Sparkplug might be concerned about hiring a woman to run his sales force of twenty-five men, so she asked her ex-boss to include her Navy experience. Also, her past sales performance was given specific documentation for maximum credibility. Finally, all of this was done briefly and to the point.

In this example, both parties know each other through the publishing business:

Mr. Anthony Deadline, President
Variety Publishing Co.
385 State Street
Chicago, Illinois
Dear Tony:

I understand you are considering hiring Alan Allstar as associate editor of Show Business and would like my professional assessment of him.

As you know, Alan was with us at Cinema for six years until 1982. During that time he progressed from copyboy to assistant business editor. One of Alan's talents that served us so well here was his uncanny ability to anticipate the news and get the jump on the competition. That talent could serve you well in your current battle with Spotlight.

Al seems to be a much stronger person since his involvement in AA. I understand that it's been over two years since he's had a drink. It's great when someone does a turnaround like that and goes on to help others.

So, Tony, I couldn't endorse Alan more strongly for your opening.

Best regards,
Bob

This letter shows how an applicant's abilities can be analyzed to highlight a specific quality that is particularly suited to the job. And while it might appear strange for Bob to bring up Alan's drinking problem, it was generally known in the entertainment-magazine field that Alan had been hitting the bottle. The frank acknowledgment that

Alan had overcome the problem turned a weakness into a strength. Recognizing negatives and dealing with them head on can defuse them and add credibility to your overall personal assessment.

Personal recommendations or character references for admissions to schools, camps, co-op buildings, or clubs require slightly different approaches. Here personal and social characteristics and civic or charitable contributions replace the professional attributes stressed in job recommendations.

Let's take a typical example, drafted by a prospective tenant applying for a cooperative apartment in a new high-rise building. Sent out by his best friend and former college roommate, who was already an owner and resident in the building, it dealt with several concerns voiced when the applicant and his wife appeared before members of the Co-op Owners' Board.

*Mr. Sam Snooty, President*
*Board of Governors*
*Haughty Towers*
*Park & Broad Streets*
*San Francisco, California*
*Dear Sam:*

> *It gives me the greatest pleasure to recommend my college roommate and friend of twenty years, George Goodfellow, and his delightful family as prospective owners of duplex 14B in Haughty Towers. George and Inga are just the type of people to facilitate our building's transition to a more youthful*

*ownership body when so many of our older residents are putting their units up for sale.*

*Not only is George highly successful in his own right, but Inga has money of her own through her family, the Bonniers of the Swedish light bulb fortune. Their financial resources, plus her work as an interior decorator, guarantee that the apartment, balcony, and small foyer they share with 14A will be maintained in impeccable taste. The rest of the building could also benefit from their ideas and generosity.*

*When we were neighbors, as newlyweds in Greenwich Village the Goodfellows organized and ran a successful block beautification association. We can expect similar involvement here.*

*Their five children have been raised in the European tradition and are bright, well behaved, and good with adults. Thanks to Inga's Swedish connection, her family here has access to qualified household help so that the children are well supervised at all times.*

*Thus, on the grounds of financial and social desirability, creative attitude toward their living environment, and appealing youngsters, I lend my unqualified endorsement to the Goodfellows.*

*Let's hope we can soon welcome this attractive couple into our co-op family.*

*Sincerely,*
*Frank Friendly, Jr.*

In his letter, Frank successfully addressed the issues George and Inga told him had been raised by one of the more conservative co-op owners: the number of children, the fact that Inga was "foreign," and, worse yet, that she worked.

In writing a school or camp recommendation for a young person, it is often advisable to enlist the parents' aid. Many teenagers, due to the pack mentality that bonds them into a look-alike, think-alike, and don't-dare-to-be-different sameness with their peers, become almost inarticulate when asked to expand on their own achievements or special characteristics.

A proud parent will have a far better fix on the kid's good qualities, as well as on those the school is looking for. Here's a letter written for the daughter of her best friend by a West Coast alumna of one of the Seven Sisters colleges. Though a generous financial supporter of her alma mater, Betsy Bluestocking hadn't revisited the campus since graduation. She composed her reference after a lengthy talk with her friend.

*Dean Isabel Intellect, Ph.D.*
*Dean of Admissions*
*Vassar College*
*Poughkeepsie, N.Y.*
*Dear Dean Intellect:*

*As one of a handful of astronomy majors back in the fifties, I have avidly followed Vassar's leadership in the field through the college bulletin. Though distance has prevented my seeing the new astronomy building and telescope that were a special fund-raising project* of mine, I've enjoyed the next-best thing. That was an enthusiastic report from Stella Stargazer about a recent campus visit and admissions interview. Stella is applying for the class of 1990.

I want to give my unqualified endorsement to this outstanding young woman in her application for early admission at Vassar.

Academically, Stella is a star with SAT scores and a school record that suggest she will be academically productive at the college. Beyond that, she is a well-rounded person whose Beverly Hills High extracurricular activities included service as photo editor of the yearbook as well as founding the Astrology Club.

She was named MVP in three sports her junior year and is president of the senior class. Stella does volunteer work at the local hospital, and babysits summers to earn spending money. She is a charming girl with a good sense of humor.

In line with Vassar's goals to broaden its student body representation, especially from the West Coast, I urge early acceptance of Stella. I'm sure both she and Vassar will benefit.

Cordially,
Betsy

Betsy had pushed all the important academic and extracurricular buttons on Stella's behalf, as well as adding a personal appraisal. At the same time, she reminded the dean of her past support and demonstrated her awareness of current admissions policies regarding West Coast recruitment. This gave Vassar two self-interest reasons for accepting Stella over other equally qualified candidates.

This chapter wouldn't be complete if it didn't address one awkward issue often faced in connection with business or social references. What if you don't feel that the candidate deserves the job recommendation? Or you can't in all honesty help him get into your old school, society, or club?

Let's take the business situation. This is a two-edged sword because recommending someone you don't know well enough or you feel is unqualified could ultimately damage your own reputation for good judgment. What's more, you're not giving either the organization or the applicant a break. The later consequences of discovering that the person was unsuitable for the job could be costly to both parties.

Yet too many people go along, however reluctantly, with a recommendation because they don't like to say no and risk hurting a colleague's feeling. Or they agree based on the misguided notion that they're doing the applicant a favor—and sometimes (not incidentally) getting a misfit out of their own company's hair. All are shortsighted in the extreme.

Most personnel experts advise not to say *anything* in a recommendation you don't mean or can't back up. It's equally unfair to write a halfhearted appraisal without informing the applicant.

In this, as in so many of life's situations, honesty *is* the best policy. If the truth is too tough, then remember the Golden Rule. How would you like to be dealt with under similar conditions?

One busy executive I know tells recommendees he doesn't know well enough, or has doubts about, that he can't let his name be used as a reference because he's on the road so much he couldn't follow through, and the delay could spoil the candidate's chances. Another pleads press of business and says she would be glad to do it six months or a year from now. All but the most insensitive applicants get the message.

My own toughest call was a reference request from an assistant who, though exemplary in every other way, was chronically late. Since this was an issue with her prospective employer, I had to tell her that her lateness record would have to be discussed. The situation turned unpleasant when she claimed I was impeding her advancement because I didn't like her. Fortunately, I had kept the company time sheets. The upshot was that I didn't write the letter, but she got therapy to get at the root of her problem and is now a vice-president at one of the largest publishing houses in the country.

If you're reluctant to write a personal reference for, say, a club, one way to defuse a potential social bombshell is to assume the blame yourself. A respectable out: that you've proposed too many people already and the club has asked that you not nominate any more members for a while. So sometimes the most important recommendation letter you'll ever face is one you don't write!

## Putting It All Together

Writing a letter of recommendation is one of the nicest

things you can do for a person, so you want to do it right. That means checking out the job he or she wants so you can tailor your letter properly, and even making the odd phone call if it will help. Sure, it takes time, and it can even be a nuisance. So to turn a chore into a breeze and help your candidate make the grade . . .

### *Remember:*

—First, ask the applicant to draft the letter in rough.

—Talk to the applicant, a business colleague, close friend, or parent to get the facts—good and bad.

—Keep the letter straightforward, clear, and fair, and cite specifics to back you up. Generalities do not inspire confidence.

—Go for a balanced view, accentuating the positive and, if possible, turning minuses into pluses.

—Never say anything you can't prove. When in doubt, leave it out.

# CHAPTER TEN

# LETTERS OF ETIQUETTE
## HOW TO SAY THANK YOU AND OFFER CONDOLENCES

The good news is that good manners are back in. The bad news is that some of the most elementary skills of common courtesy have become a lost art. An entire generation has grown up intimidated by their ignorance of the basic forms of etiquette that came as naturally as breathing to their parents' generation.

## The Thank-You Note

Who needed *Lohengrin* and lace when you could write your own marriage vows and recite them standing barefoot in a stream? Why write Granny a thank-you note for her graduation present when you could call from school—collect, natch—and cheer the old girl up? Today the new bride sits at a loss in front of her new Tiffany notepaper. The language of the wedding gift thank-you is as mysterious to her as the ancient Egyptian hieroglyphics were before the discovery of the Rosetta stone.

Since gratitude has been dubbed the memory of the heart, it's not surprising that letters of thanks comprise 90 percent of the correspondence of good manners.

## Rules of the Game

The three most common types of thank-you letters are for gifts, hospitality (traditionally known as bread-and-butter notes), and favors. The same rules apply whether you are saying thank you for a holiday present, a dinner party, a weekend visit, a business outing, or a favor.

1. *Write your letter promptly.* Unless you are saying thanks for a wedding gift (in which case you have a year of grace, according to Emily Post), write your letter no later than ten days after the act.

2. *Be specific.* Mention the gift by name, describe the good time you had, go into some detail about the favor you so appreciate.

3. *Be sincere,* even if the purple ice bucket is still in its box. There's usually *something* kind or grateful you can say.

4. *Write your letter yourself.* Don't dictate it to your secretary to type. The recipient of your letter took the time to do something personal for you and deserves an equally personal expression of thanks.

SOME EXAMPLES

While the requirements are not difficult, writing a good thank-you isn't always easy. Not even if you were brought up, as I was, to acknowledge a gift or a party or a special favor almost before the wrapping paper is tossed away, the dinner digested, or the favor carried out. (In fact, I often wondered how Santa knew to tuck a box of notepaper in the toe of my Christmas stocking for the duty that lay ahead!)

Here's an example of the classic gift thank-you note, short and sweet:

*Dear Granny and Gramps:*

*Thank you so much for the super Sanyo cassette player. How did you know it was at the top of my list? On second thought, I can guess which little bird told you. On Christmas morning Mom passed me your present first!*

*It was a much needed gift and I love it. I'm sure you'll be glad to know I'll be using it for my language tapes at college. Thanks again, and I hope your Christmas was as much fun as ours. I hope next year we can all spend it together.*

*Love,*
*Heather*

This letter has the most important element of all— the ring of truth. That's because Heather took the trouble to be specific, right down to the brand name of the player, and included personal details that made her gratitude come alive.

A word here about money gifts. How to wax poetic and sound sincere about that least imaginative of gifts? Take the trouble to do what the giver didn't. Write and tell him/her what a wonderful whatamacallit you bought with the generous gift. Avoid the grim truth—that you paid the rent with it!

Having looked the gift horse in the mouth, let's move on to the next largest classification of thank-you notes, the bread-and-butter letter that says thanks for the hospitality. Hardly a host or hostess exists who is not more touched and gratified by the briefest note than by the longest telephone call. But be prompt! Don't let a week, at most, go by without putting pen to paper. If guests, like fish, begin to smell after three days, there is nothing less appealing than a stale bread-and-butter letter.

Lawyer Hiram Achiever and his newscaster wife, Anne, held jobs that involved considerable entertainment by clients or by higher-ups in their respective companies. Reminding themselves of the old Turkish proverb, "The courteous learns his courtesy from the discourteous," they were meticulous in writing prompt, personal bread-and-butters. Here's a typical B-and-B that speaks for itself:

*Mr. Ron Powerplay*
*Golden Triangle Development Corp.*
*Monongahela and Main Sts.*
*Pittsburgh, PA 56091*
*Dear Ron:*

> *Thank you and Judy for a super time out*
> *at the old ball game last night. Your company*

*box at Three Rivers Stadium certainly is the place to be on a hot August night, especially with the Pirates breaking that darned losing streak. And the crowning touch of meeting Willie Stargell after the game just made the evening for Hi and me.*

*The barbeque was delicious; nothing beats ribs washed down with good old Iron City! And the T-shirts with "Make the Cards Walk the Plank!" were a fun and thoughtful touch.*

*Thanks again for a great evening. We hope to see you both <u>chez nous</u> before long.*

*All the best,*
*Anne and Hi*

If gifts and hospitality merit thank-you notes, so do favors done for you by others. The closer the friendship, the more important is some form of acknowledgment of anything done beyond the call of duty. A letter is a perfect way to keep the relationship polished. Here's an example:

*Dear Jon,*

*Bet you never expected to get a real live letter from your good buddy. (Sexy postcards from Club Med, maybe?) But nothing less than a letter will do to thank you for all you did to help Patty and me move into our apartment.*

*The loan of your pickup to move our stuff from her family's and mine to the apartment was great. With both our parents being so down on our plans to live together, we were fresh out of wheels. Don't know what we would have done without your trusty truck!*

*And as if helping us get our stuff together on the coldest, wettest day of the year wasn't enough, you really blew my mind when you showed up with your paintbrush and two six-packs Friday. The rest of the gang talked about helping us. You <u>did</u> it.*

*They say a true friend is a second self. Thanks, old pal, for being that to me.*

> *As ever,*
> *Dave*

*P.S. Patty calls the color you picked for the bathroom Pepto-Bismol! But I like it. It reminds me of your eyes after one of our fraternity blowouts!*

## Letters of Condolence

Most of us find sympathy notes or letters of condolence the most difficult ones to write. There are a number of reasons for this. But none of them is any excuse for not writing those most painful but meaningful of letters.

People feel—with reason—that words are inadequate to deal with profound sorrow, or to convey a true sense of caring and comfort. They also fear not being able to come up with the right words on their own.

Honesty is the best policy, so make a virtue of necessity. In fact, confessing to being tongue-tied or at a loss for words in the face of devastating loss is one of the best ways to get you started on a sympathy letter, as in: "I know that a letter is of little comfort at a time like this, but . . . " or "If I could only find the words to tell you what my heart feels for you at this moment."

In one of the great sympathy letters of all time, written to Mrs. Lydia Bixby of Boston, Massachusetts, upon the loss of her five sons in the Civil War, Abraham Lincoln expressed this common sentiment well: "I feel how weak and fruitless must be any word of mine which shall attempt to beguile you from a loss so overwhelming."

The second hang-up about writing generally afflicts people who themselves may not have suffered the loss of anyone close. They feel helpless and unable to identify with the sorrow of a friend or relative. So they're hesitant to write and put their foot in it, so to speak.

Perhaps the most common cause for our difficulty in composing sympathy notes is a misunderstanding of the nature of the grief process itself. Most of us believe, quite correctly, that grief is a private affair, so we are reluctant to put pen to paper for fear of intruding. But nothing could be further from the truth.

That's because a sympathy note is *less* intrusive than face-to-face or phone communication. Yet it provides written evidence of compassion to be read in private at a time when emotional support is so important. And because a letter can be taken out and read again, it may help the bereaved work his or her way through the several stages of grief.

In the preliminary phase of shock/numbness/denial, a letter helps underscore the reality of loss while seeking to assuage it. During the next stages of anger/self-pity/despair/loneliness, the letter gives tangible evidence of the concern of others as well as giving the solace of positive memories of the late relative or friend. And the

141

guilt felt by most survivors about all those things left unsaid or undone can be addressed.

That's why it's so important to include in a note an acknowledgment of the positive role that the recipient and/or other family members played in the life or final illness of the departed. As Thomas Mann so wisely said, "A man's dying is more the survivors' affair than his own."

To someone who may be regretting not having lived closer to a parent, what balm there can be in a statement like: "How much comfort you and the family must derive from the obvious joy your mother displayed on those happy occasions when you were able to visit her from so far away."

Then, as the mourner works toward the final stage of the grief process—acceptance and getting on with life—a sympathy letter can be shared with other family members, providing a common bond of comfort and recollections of the deceased in happier days.

Lastly, we dread writing sympathy notes because it reminds us that we're all going to die someday. And that's not a pleasant thought.

Okay, so we are agreed. No matter what else you do when someone dies—whether you call on the phone or in person, send flowers, food, or a contribution to a favorite charity, attend the wake, the funeral, or the memorial service—a condolence letter is a must. And forget those store-bought sympathy cards. They are a commercial cop-out and absolutely no substitute for the real thing.

## Rules of the Game

There are four basic areas you should cover in a condolence note:

1. *Acknowledge the death.* If you can't bring yourself to use the word, substitute "your loss" or "the sad news about ———."

2. *Praise the departed* with as personal a touch as possible.

3. *Include an "at a loss for words" sentence* (optional) and any guilt-relieving statement you wish to make.

4. *Close with reassurance* and, if you like, an offer to help. The former can range from a general one—"Please know our sympathies, our love, and our thoughts are with you"—to something highly specific—"I'll call to see when I can drop off a casserole." Avoid the vague or open-ended "Please let us know if we can do anything" or "Call me when you feel up to it." These merely add to the pressure on the already burdened recipient by putting the ball in his or her court.

What about length? A condolence note can be as brief as a couple of sentences and still cover the necessary bases. Or it can be somewhat longer if the relationship warrants. As to timing, the sooner the better. But some of the most helpful and healing letters I received after the death of my parents (who lived a continent away) came months later from people who were delayed in getting the news. So you're not off the hook if you miss the first

143

opportunity. In fact, as the survivor works through his or her grief, letters sharing memories are especially helpful.

SOME EXAMPLES

Let's look at some sympathy letters, in order of the degree of intimacy with the recipient and written under varying circumstances. Here's one to a business acquaintance on the death of his father:

> *Dear Tod:*
>
> *We were saddened to read in this week's Industry Today of your father's sudden death. He and his contributions to your company, the business world, and our whole community were greatly admired by all who knew him.*
>
> *Words are a small comfort at a time like this, but it may help to know that you have the warm wishes and sympathy of your family's many friends. The close father-son bond you shared has been an example to all of us.*
>
> *My wife joins me in sending our heartfelt condolences to you and your family.*
>
> > *Sincerely,*
> > *Bill*

Here is one to a social acquaintance who lost her husband:

> *Dear Alice:*
>
> *Bill and I just heard your sad news. Words seem so inadequate to express our feelings in your time of grief and loss.*
>
> *We'll always remember Jack with such affection for his ready smile and willingness to lend a helping hand. He'll be sorely missed by his many friends in Hometown.*
>
> *Please know that you and the family, who meant so much to Jack and gave him such happiness always, are in our thoughts and prayers.*
>
> > *Affectionately,*
> > *Jane*

Note that both letters come right to the point without beating around the bush with euphemisms. Ours is a culture that prefers to deny the final fact of death. Phrases like "passed on," "gone to his great reward," or "to a better life" beg the issue and should be avoided.

The personal touch is of necessity limited by the fact that the relationships were not that close, but the references are still specific enough to be consoling.

Finally, both letters close with the appropriate expression of what action the sender feels capable of taking, i.e., sending condolences or simply saying a prayer.

Next is the longer and more personal letter to an

intimate friend whose mother has died after a long struggle with cancer:

*Darling Phoebe:*

*We were devastated to hear that your mother's valiant battle has ended. We grieve with and for you on your loss of that wonderful lady.*

*Much as one is relieved that the suffering of a dear one is over, nothing can alter the grief that the death of a beloved parent brings. As that chapter of her life ends, it also brings to a close an era for you. My heart aches for you.*

*You can take great comfort in the knowledge that you, Phil, and the kids always did so much to make her life rich and full. And the loving care you all gave her during her last illness must have greatly eased that dreadful time for her.*

*Even as I write this, I can't help thinking of your mom the way I knew and loved her best—eyes bright, head cocked, drawing out someone else about themselves. She truly had the gift of an unselfish interest in others that made her one of the most interesting people I have ever known.*

*Remembering your mom, I'm reminded of what the late Stanley Holloway, the British actor who starred in My Fair Lady, was reported to have said in a note to the wife of a dear friend who died: "Paradise is a better place for his presence." True—and we all are poorer for your mother's death.*

*John joins me in sending our sympathy to you all. We'll be calling you to see how many out-of-towners we can put up for the memorial service next month.*

*Dearest love,*
*Charity*

The letter contained all the requisite ingredients. It also avoided the one trap people tend to fall into when the death follows a long or agonizing illness—saying that it was a blessing. Even if true, such statements are reserved strictly for the bereaved to make first.

## Putting It All Together

Good manners are the Golden Rule in action. You can write wonderful letters expressing gratitude or sympathy if you put yourself in the recipient's place. Then the letter will have the hallmark of considerate and courteous behavior. It will sound as if it comes from the heart—because it does.

### Remember:

—Be prompt.
—Write personally. *A printed card is never a substitute*. If you must keep the greeting card industry in business—or if you've found one that is simply irresistible—send it as well as, not instead of, your letter.
—Be specific. Vague generalities are the lazy man's

way. What's more, they sound insincere. Taking the trouble to add a telling detail not only shows you care, but adds the ring of truth to your gesture.

And as you take pen, rather than phone, in hand, remember what Ralph Waldo Emerson wrote: "Manners are the happy way of doing things. . . . If they are superficial, so are the dewdrops, which gave such depth to the morning meadow."